AMAZING WORLD WAR II STORIES

NAVAJO CODE TALKERS

TOP SECRET MESSENGERS OF WORLD WAR II

by Blake Hoena
illustrated by Marcel P. Massegú

Consultant:
Tim Solie
Adjunct Professor of History
Minnesota State University, Mankato
Mankato, Minnesota

CAPSTONE PRESS
a capstone imprint

Graphic Library is published by Capstone Press,
1710 Roe Crest Drive, North Mankato, Minnesota 56003
www.capstonepub.com

Library of Congress Cataloging-in-Publication data is available on the Library of Congress website.
Names: Hoena, B. A., author. | Perez Massegú, Marcel, illustrator.
Title: Navajo code talkers : top secret messengers of World War II / by Blake Hoena ; illustrated by Marcel P. Massegú.
Description: North Mankato, Minnesota : Capstone Press, a Capstone imprint, [2020] | Series: Graphic library. Amazing World War II stories | Audience: Ages 8–14. | Audience: Grades 4–6. | Includes bibliographical references and index.
Identifiers: LCCN 2019005961| ISBN 9781543573145 (library binding) | ISBN 9781543575491 (paperback) | ISBN 9781543573183 (ebook pdf)
Subjects: LCSH: World War, 1939–1945—Cryptography—Juvenile literature. | Navajo code talkers—Juvenile literature. | Navajo language—Juvenile literature. | World War, 1939–1945—Participation, Indian—Juvenile literature. | United States. Marine Corps—Indian troops—History—20th century—Juvenile literature.
Classification: LCC D810.C88 H64 2020 | DDC 940.54/8673—dc23
LC record available at https://lccn.loc.gov/2019005961

Summary: In graphic novel format, tells the amazing story of the Navajo Code Talkers and how they created and used an unbreakable code to help U.S. forces fight and win several battles in World War II.

EDITOR
Aaron J. Sautter

ART DIRECTOR
Nathan Gassman

DESIGNER
Ted Williams

PRODUCTION SPECIALIST
Katy LaVigne

Design Elements by Shutterstock/Guenter Albers

The spellings of Navajo code words in this book are accurate to the World War II era, but may differ from modern spellings.

All internet sites appearing in back matter were available and accurate when this book was sent to press.

Direct quotation appears in ***bold italicized text*** on the following page:
Page 28: from "Remarks by the President in a Ceremony Honoring the Navajo Code Talkers," by The White House, Washington, D.C., July 26, 2001 (https://georgewbush-whitehouse.archives.gov/news/releases/2001/07/20010726-5.html).

Printed in the United States 4931

TABLE OF CONTENTS

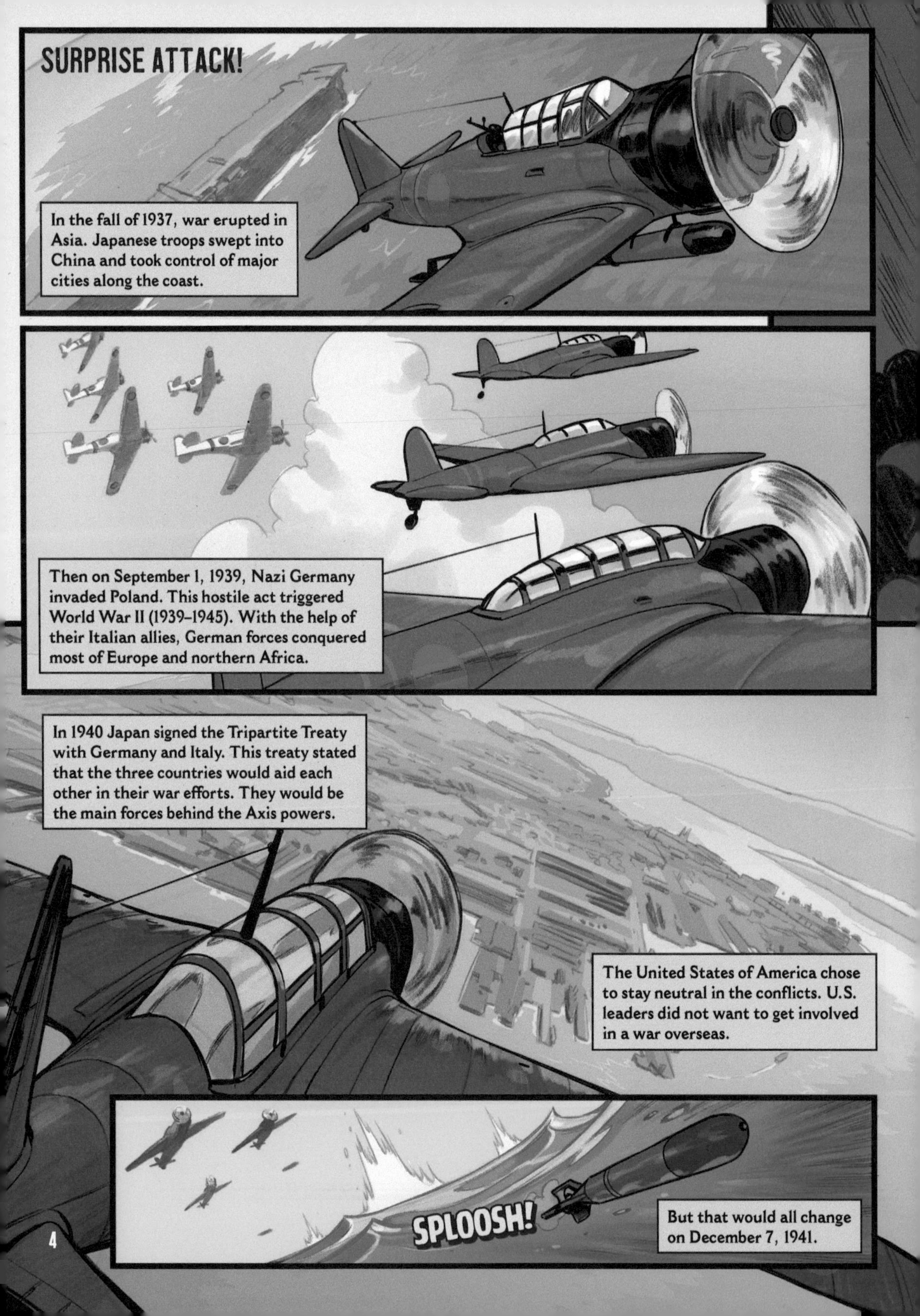
SURPRISE ATTACK!
In the fall of 1937, war erupted in Asia. Japanese troops swept into China and took control of major cities along the coast.
Then on September 1, 1939, Nazi Germany invaded Poland. This hostile act triggered World War II (1939–1945). With the help of their Italian allies, German forces conquered most of Europe and northern Africa.
In 1940 Japan signed the Tripartite Treaty with Germany and Italy. This treaty stated that the three countries would aid each other in their war efforts. They would be the main forces behind the Axis powers.
The United States of America chose to stay neutral in the conflicts. U.S. leaders did not want to get involved in a war overseas.
SPLOOSH!
But that would all change on December 7, 1941.

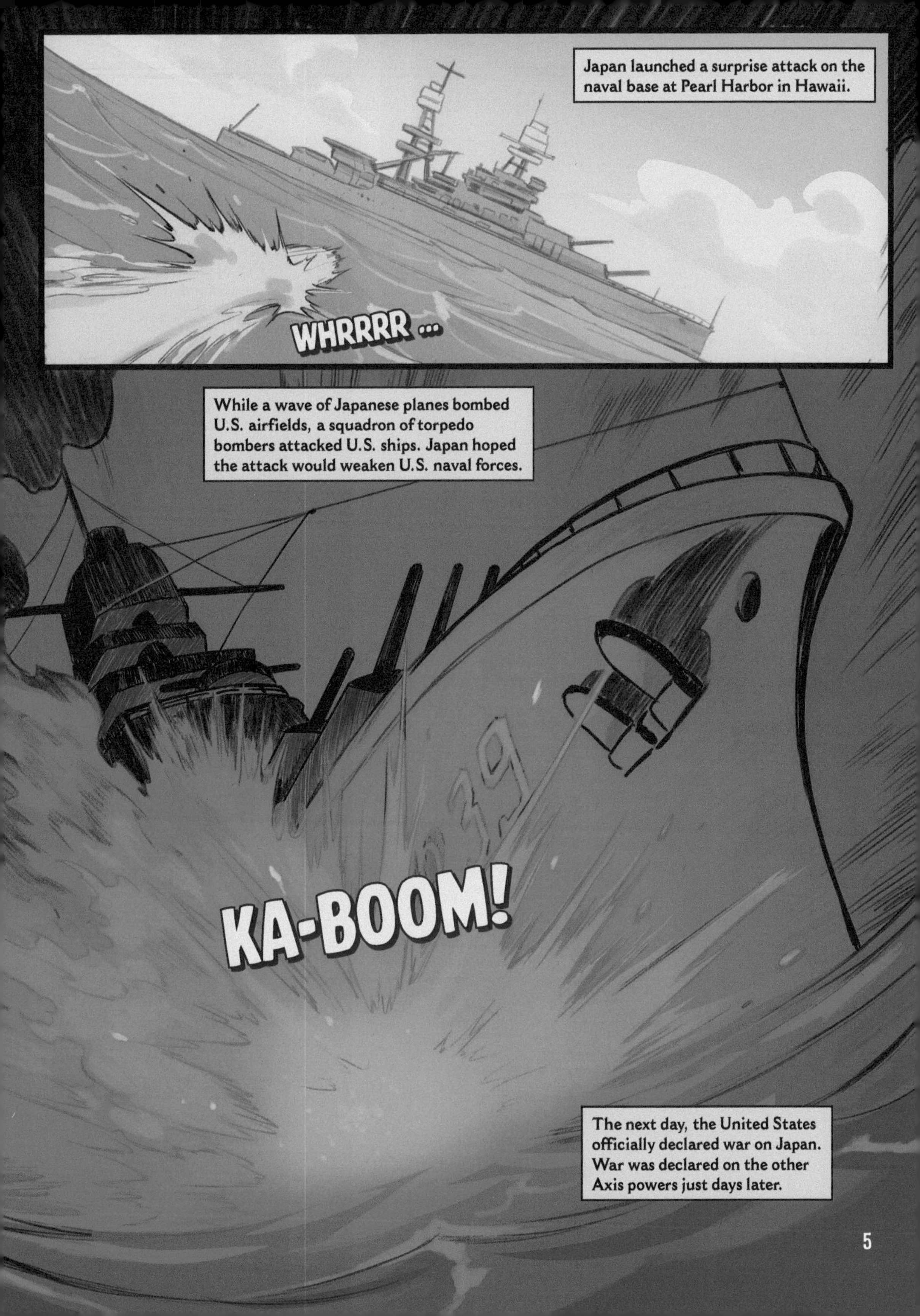
Japan launched a surprise attack on the naval base at Pearl Harbor in Hawaii.
WHRRRR ...
While a wave of Japanese planes bombed U.S. airfields, a squadron of torpedo bombers attacked U.S. ships. Japan hoped the attack would weaken U.S. naval forces.
KA-BOOM!
The next day, the United States officially declared war on Japan. War was declared on the other Axis powers just days later.

CREATING A NEW CODE

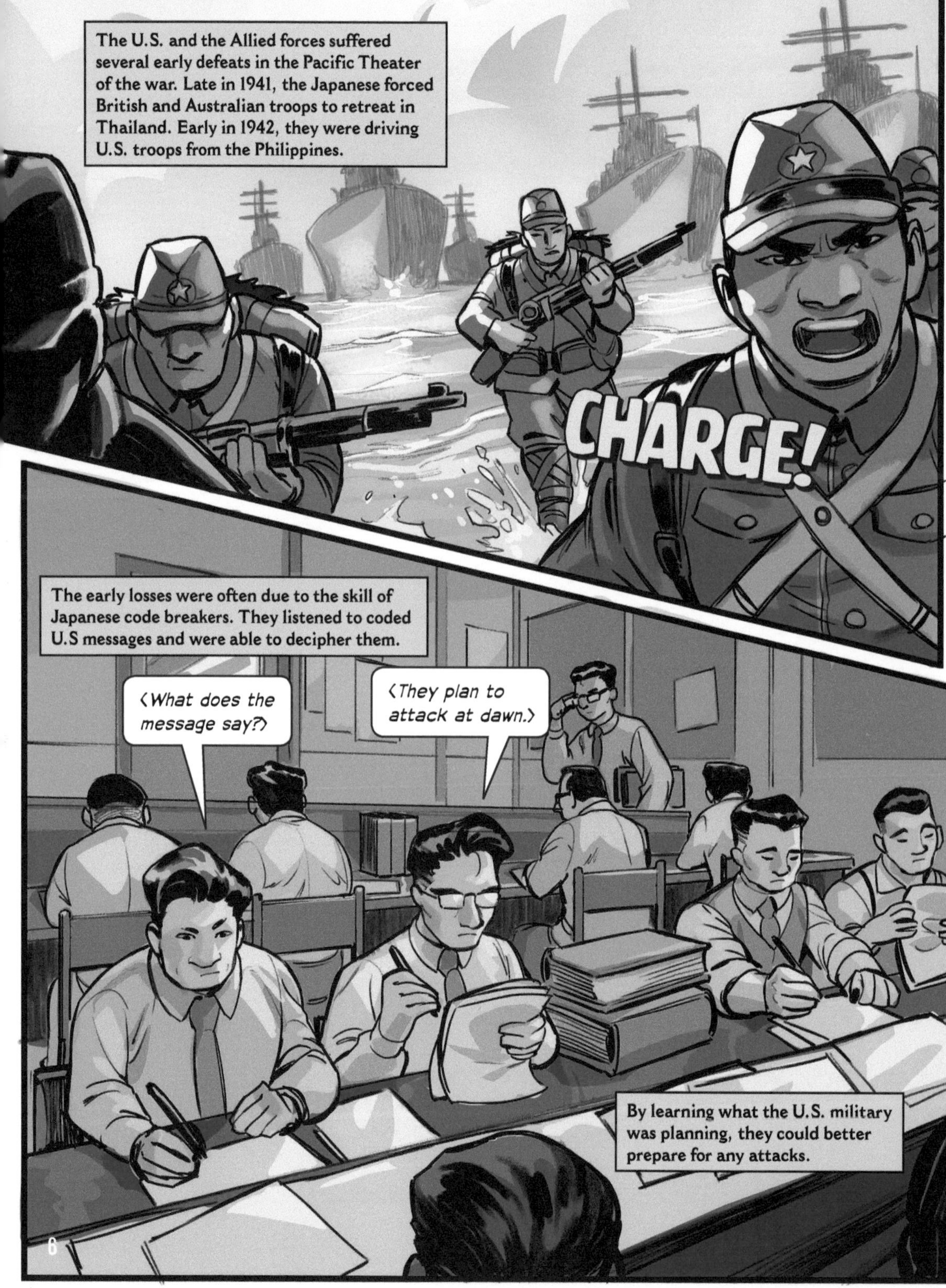
The U.S. and the Allied forces suffered several early defeats in the Pacific Theater of the war. Late in 1941, the Japanese forced British and Australian troops to retreat in Thailand. Early in 1942, they were driving U.S. troops from the Philippines.
CHARGE!
The early losses were often due to the skill of Japanese code breakers. They listened to coded U.S messages and were able to decipher them.
‹What does the message say?›
‹They plan to attack at dawn.›
By learning what the U.S. military was planning, they could better prepare for any attacks.

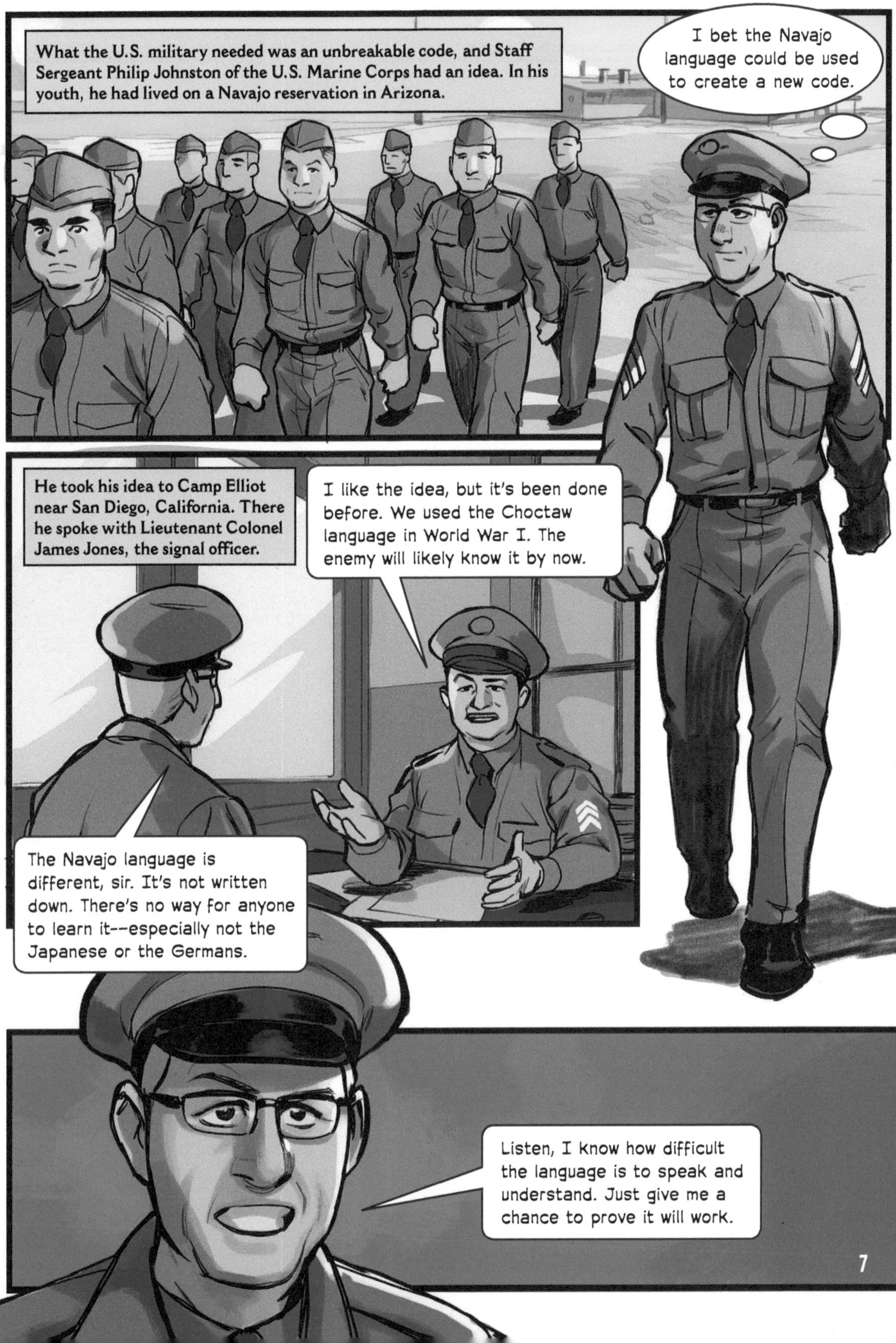
What the U.S. military needed was an unbreakable code, and Staff Sergeant Philip Johnston of the U.S. Marine Corps had an idea. In his youth, he had lived on a Navajo reservation in Arizona.
I bet the Navajo language could be used to create a new code.
He took his idea to Camp Elliot near San Diego, California. There he spoke with Lieutenant Colonel James Jones, the signal officer.
I like the idea, but it's been done before. We used the Choctaw language in World War I. The enemy will likely know it by now.
The Navajo language is different, sir. It's not written down. There's no way for anyone to learn it--especially not the Japanese or the Germans.
Listen, I know how difficult the language is to speak and understand. Just give me a chance to prove it will work.

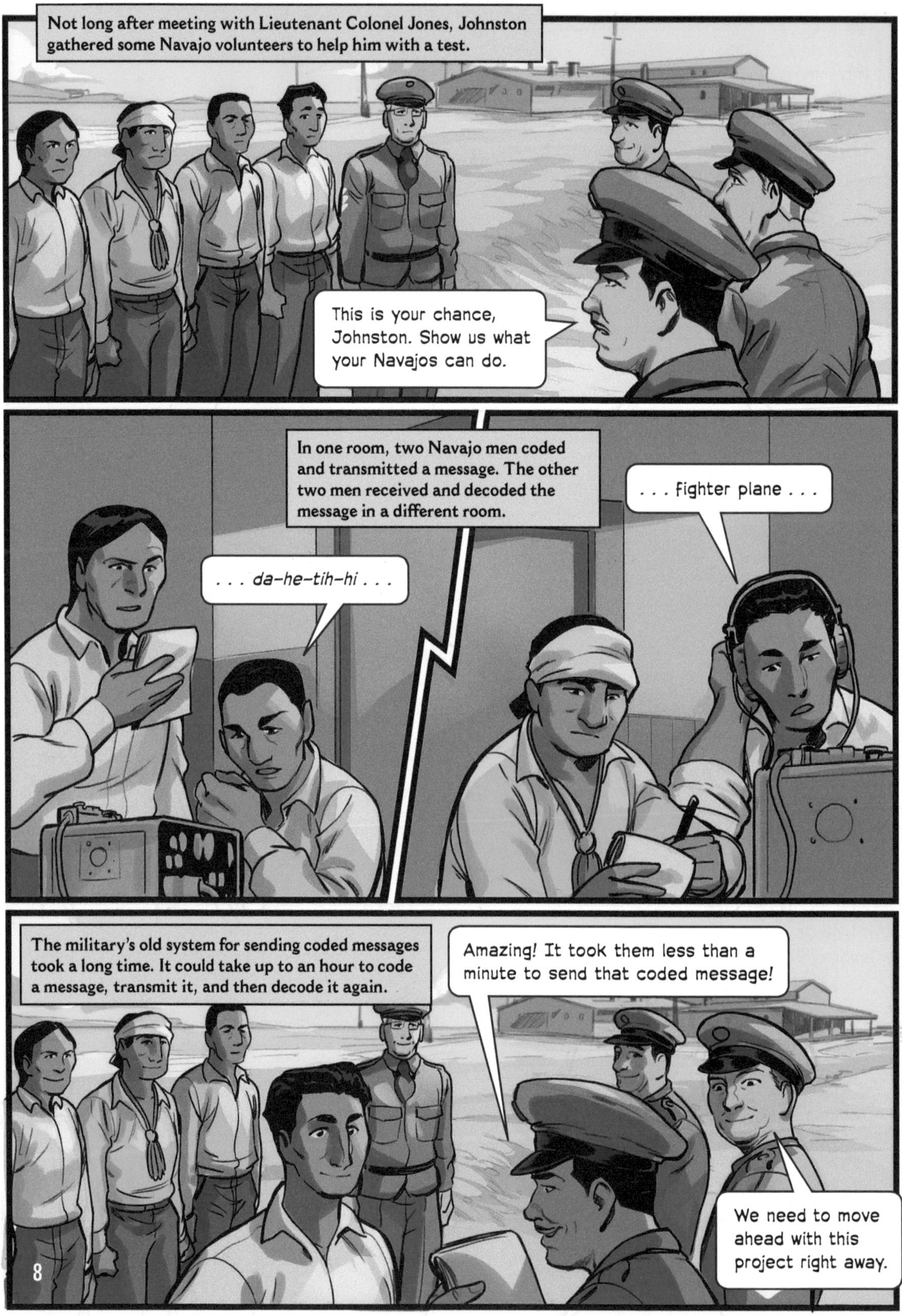
Not long after meeting with Lieutenant Colonel Jones, Johnston gathered some Navajo volunteers to help him with a test.
This is your chance, Johnston. Show us what your Navajos can do.
In one room, two Navajo men coded and transmitted a message. The other two men received and decoded the message in a different room.
. . . da-he-tih-hi . . .
. . . fighter plane . . .
The military's old system for sending coded messages took a long time. It could take up to an hour to code a message, transmit it, and then decode it again.
Amazing! It took them less than a minute to send that coded message!
We need to move ahead with this project right away.

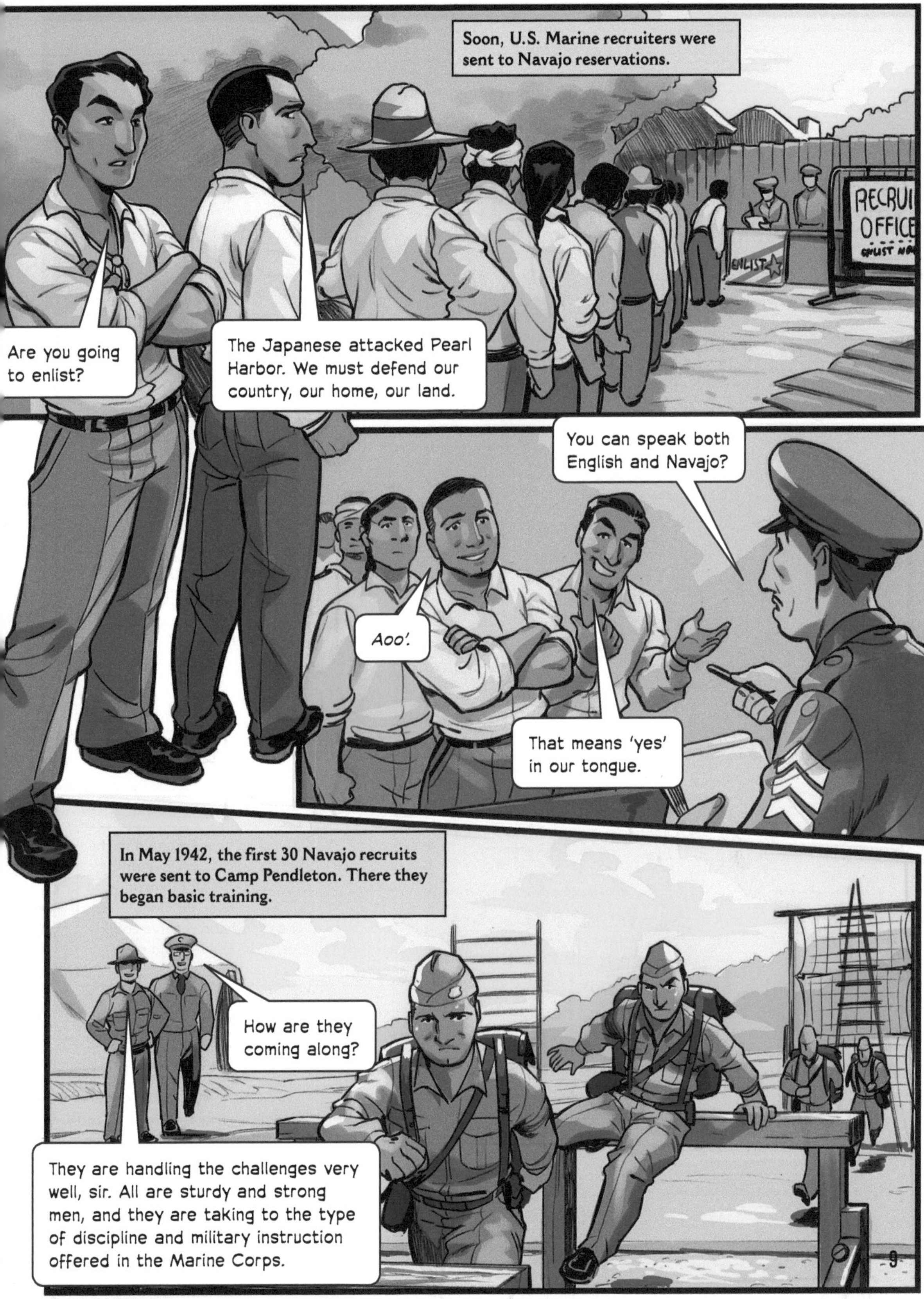
Soon, U.S. Marine recruiters were sent to Navajo reservations.
RECRUI
OFFICE
ENLIST
Are you going to enlist?
The Japanese attacked Pearl Harbor. We must defend our country, our home, our land.
You can speak both English and Navajo?
Aoo'.
That means 'yes' in our tongue.
In May 1942, the first 30 Navajo recruits were sent to Camp Pendleton. There they began basic training.
How are they coming along?
They are handling the challenges very well, sir. All are sturdy and strong men, and they are taking to the type of discipline and military instruction offered in the Marine Corps.

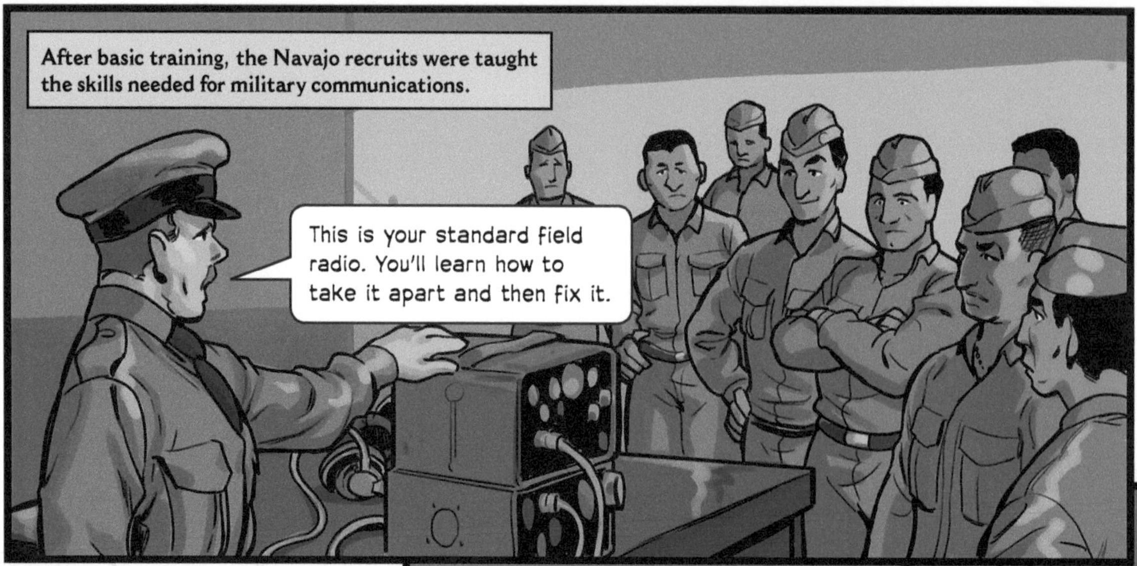
After basic training, the Navajo recruits were taught the skills needed for military communications.
This is your standard field radio. You'll learn how to take it apart and then fix it.

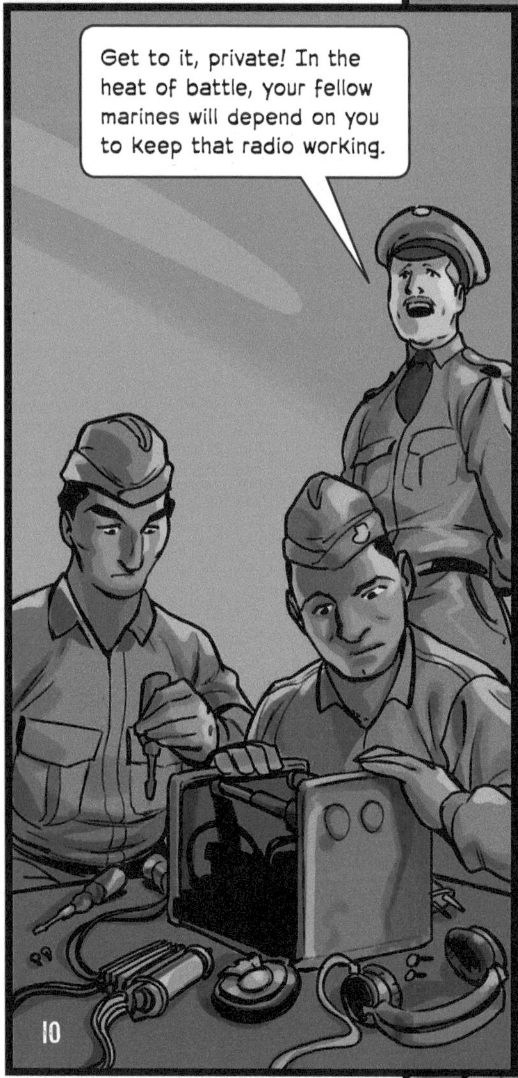
Get to it, private! In the heat of battle, your fellow marines will depend on you to keep that radio working.

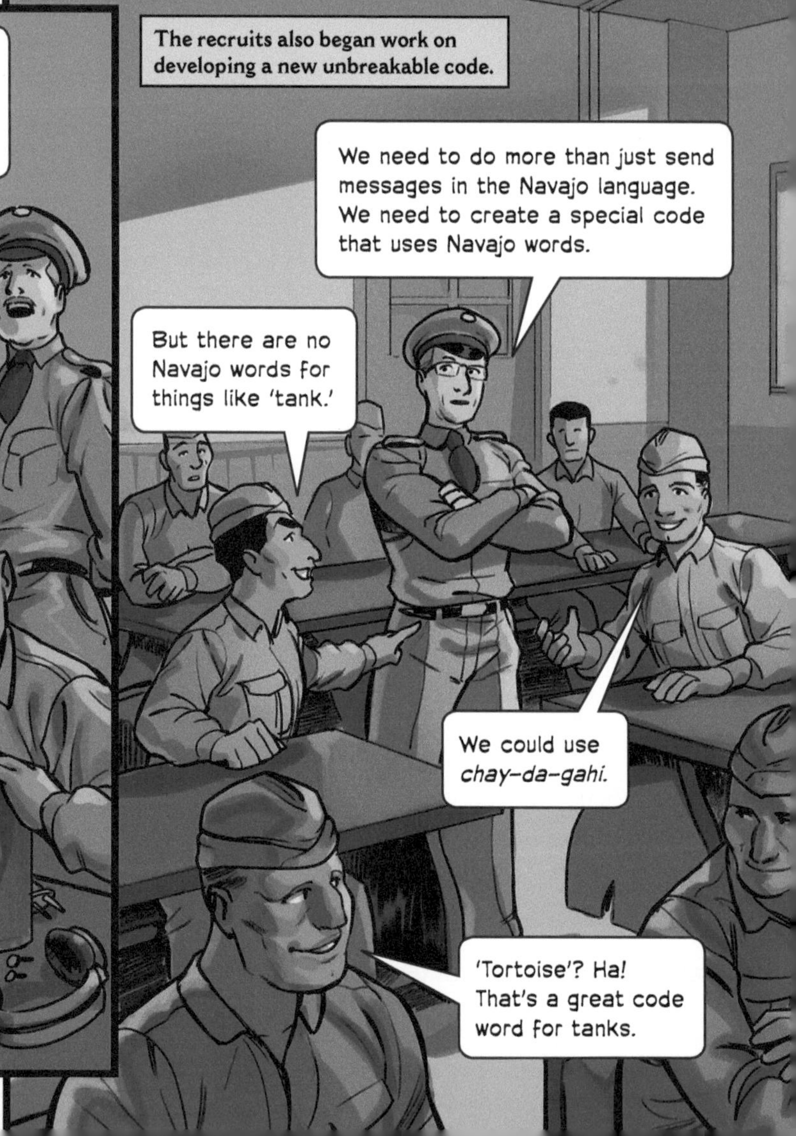
The recruits also began work on developing a new unbreakable code.
We need to do more than just send messages in the Navajo language. We need to create a special code that uses Navajo words.
But there are no Navajo words for things like 'tank.'
We could use *chay-da-gahi*.
'Tortoise'? Ha! That's a great code word for tanks.

The Navajo started with a dictionary of more than 200 code words. All of the words had to be memorized during their training. They also created a coded alphabet to spell out other words. More words would be added later.

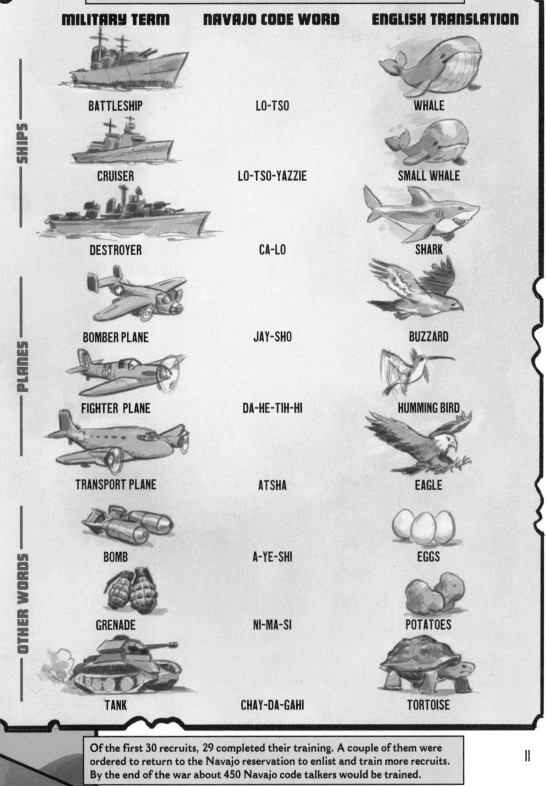

	MILITARY TERM	NAVAJO CODE WORD	ENGLISH TRANSLATION
SHIPS	BATTLESHIP	LO-TSO	WHALE
SHIPS	CRUISER	LO-TSO-YAZZIE	SMALL WHALE
SHIPS	DESTROYER	CA-LO	SHARK
PLANES	BOMBER PLANE	JAY-SHO	BUZZARD
PLANES	FIGHTER PLANE	DA-HE-TIH-HI	HUMMING BIRD
PLANES	TRANSPORT PLANE	ATSHA	EAGLE
OTHER WORDS	BOMB	A-YE-SHI	EGGS
OTHER WORDS	GRENADE	NI-MA-SI	POTATOES
OTHER WORDS	TANK	CHAY-DA-GAHI	TORTOISE

Of the first 30 recruits, 29 completed their training. A couple of them were ordered to return to the Navajo reservation to enlist and train more recruits. By the end of the war about 450 Navajo code talkers would be trained.

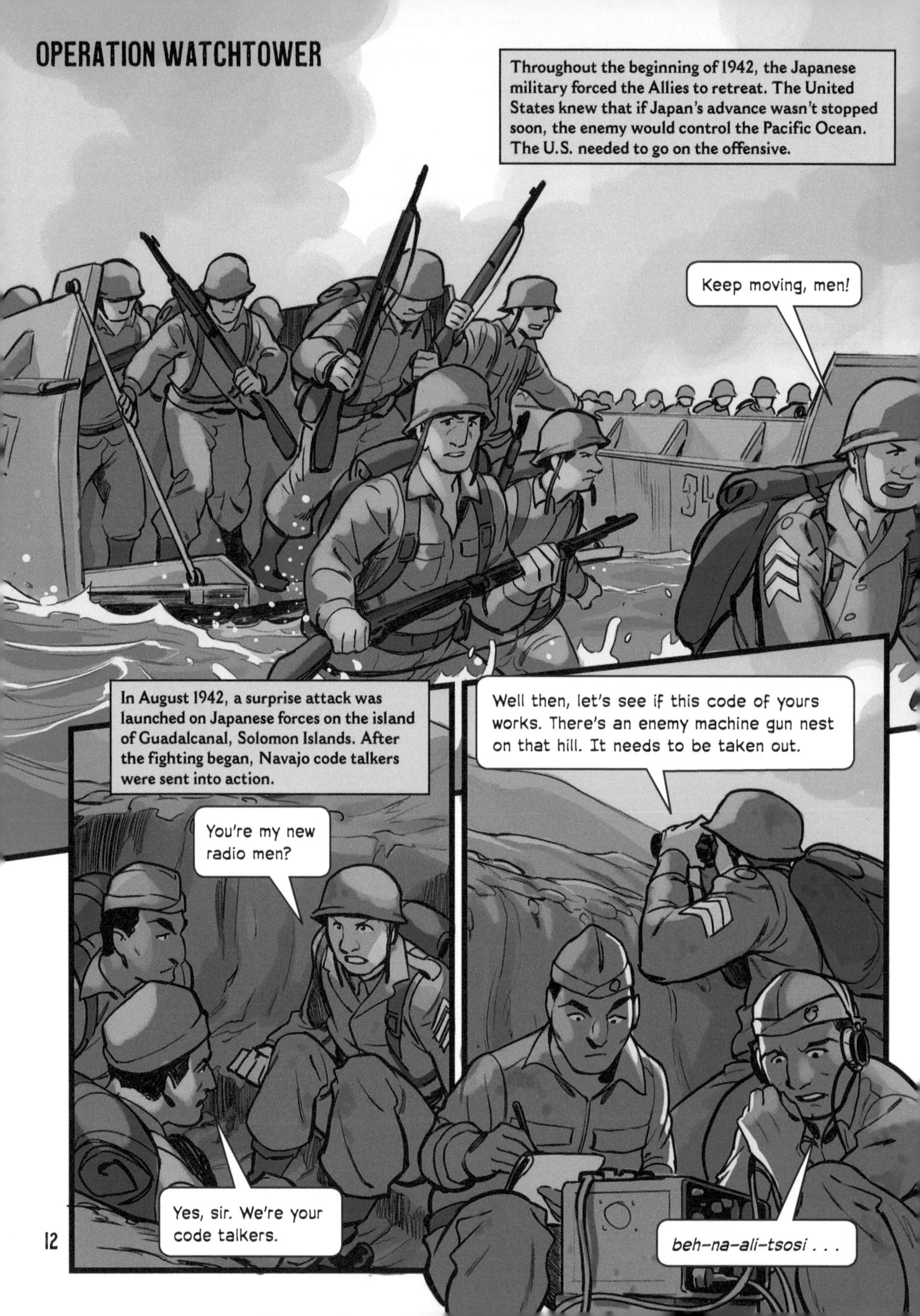
OPERATION WATCHTOWER
Throughout the beginning of 1942, the Japanese military forced the Allies to retreat. The United States knew that if Japan's advance wasn't stopped soon, the enemy would control the Pacific Ocean. The U.S. needed to go on the offensive.
Keep moving, men!
In August 1942, a surprise attack was launched on Japanese forces on the island of Guadalcanal, Solomon Islands. After the fighting began, Navajo code talkers were sent into action.
You're my new radio men?
Yes, sir. We're your code talkers.
Well then, let's see if this code of yours works. There's an enemy machine gun nest on that hill. It needs to be taken out.
beh-na-ali-tsosi . . .

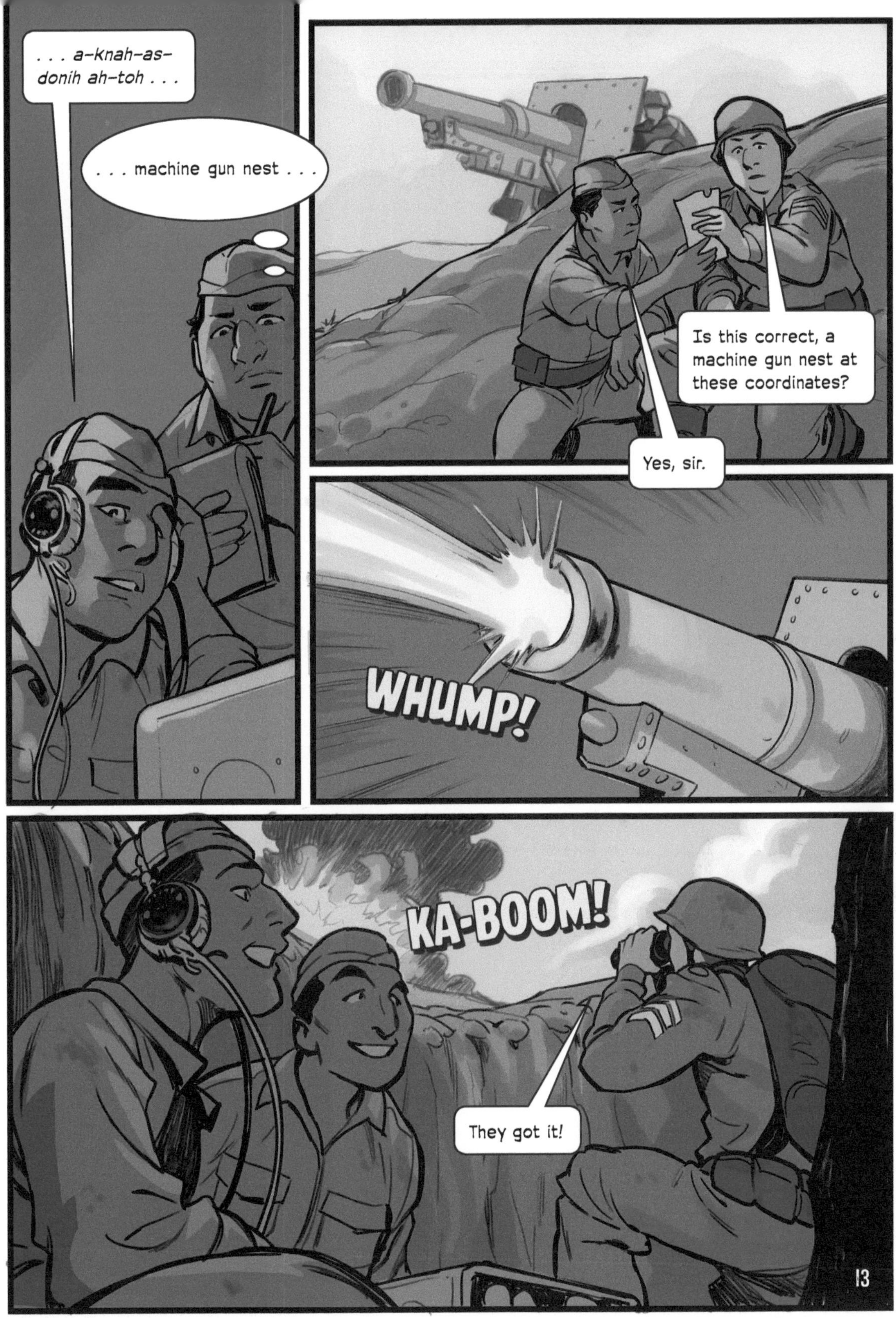

. . . a-knah-as-donih ah-toh . . .
. . . machine gun nest . . .
Is this correct, a machine gun nest at these coordinates?
Yes, sir.
WHUMP!
KA-BOOM!
They got it!

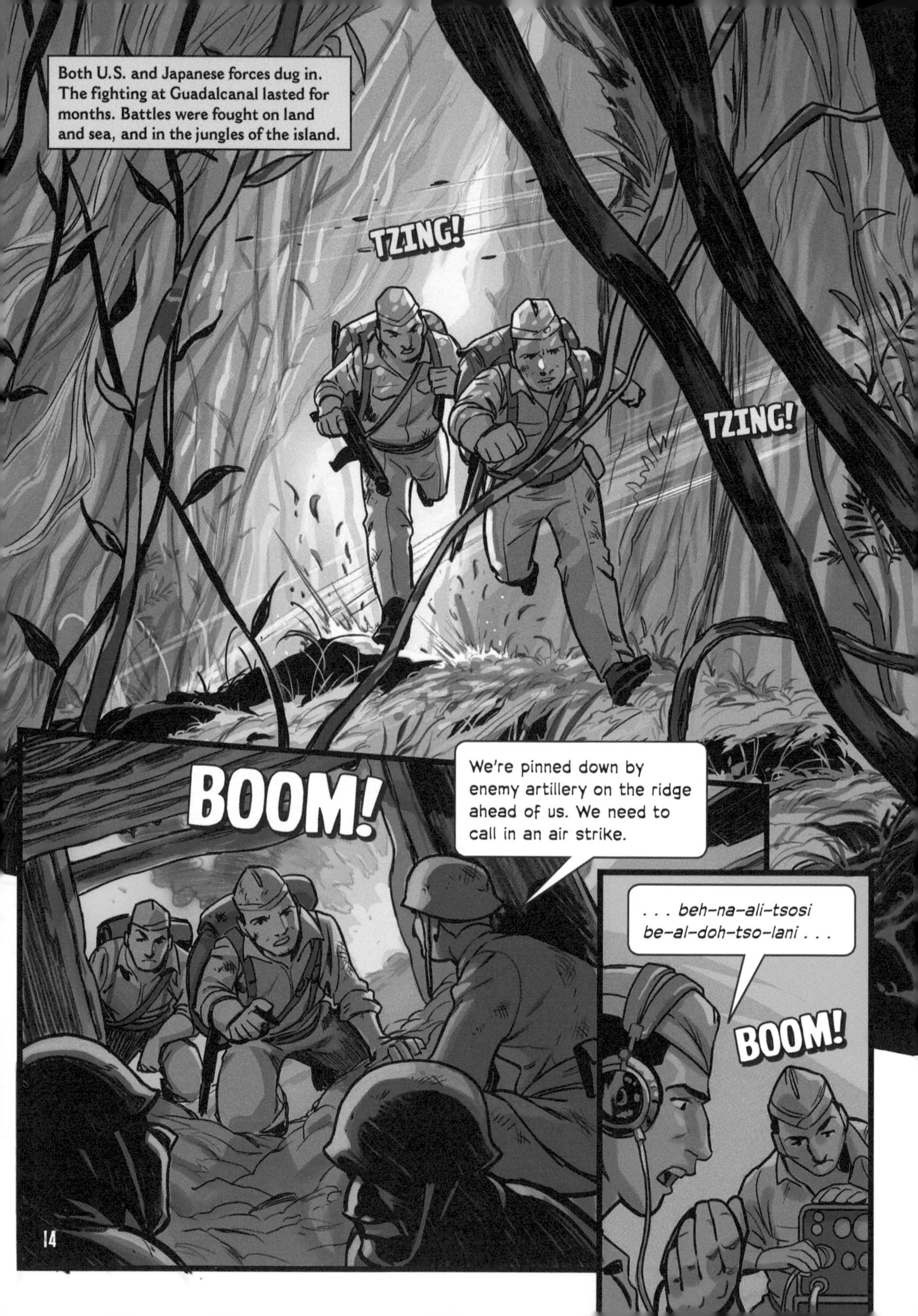
Both U.S. and Japanese forces dug in. The fighting at Guadalcanal lasted for months. Battles were fought on land and sea, and in the jungles of the island.
TZING!
TZING!
BOOM!
We're pinned down by enemy artillery on the ridge ahead of us. We need to call in an air strike.
. . . beh-na-ali-tsosi be-al-doh-tso-lani . . .
BOOM!

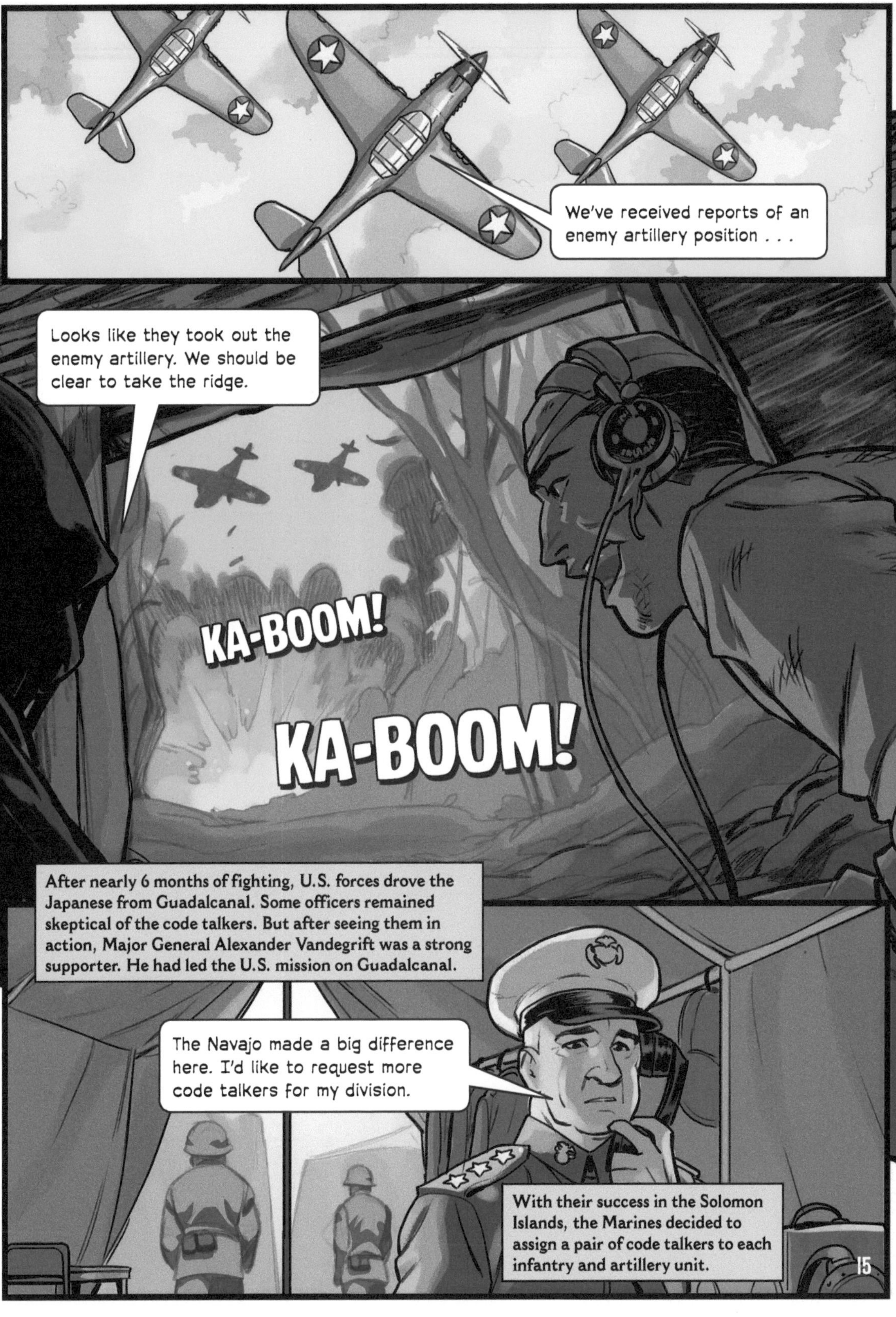
We've received reports of an enemy artillery position . . .
Looks like they took out the enemy artillery. We should be clear to take the ridge.
KA-BOOM!
KA-BOOM!
After nearly 6 months of fighting, U.S. forces drove the Japanese from Guadalcanal. Some officers remained skeptical of the code talkers. But after seeing them in action, Major General Alexander Vandegrift was a strong supporter. He had led the U.S. mission on Guadalcanal.
The Navajo made a big difference here. I'd like to request more code talkers for my division.
With their success in the Solomon Islands, the Marines decided to assign a pair of code talkers to each infantry and artillery unit.

ISLAND HOPPING

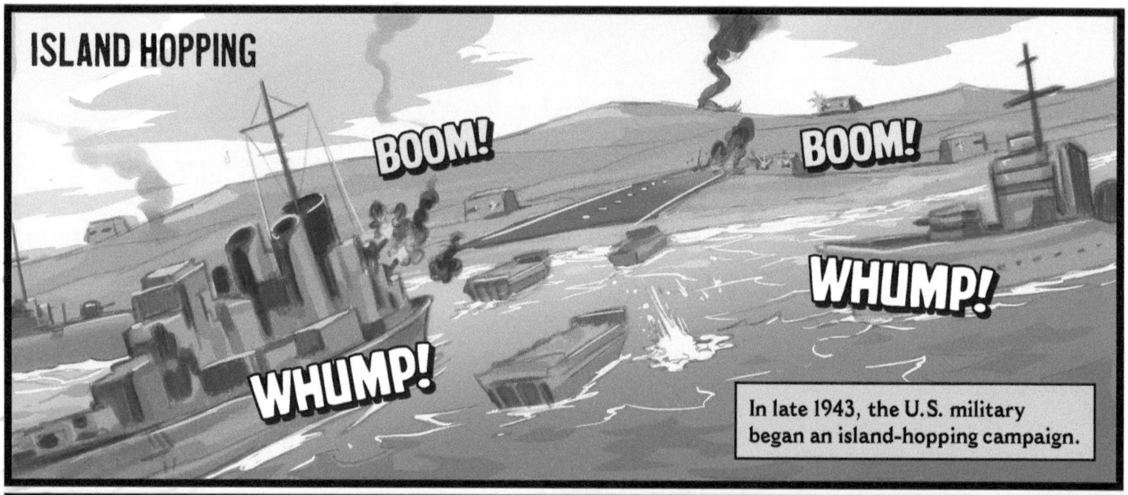
BOOM!
BOOM!
WHUMP!
WHUMP!
In late 1943, the U.S. military began an island-hopping campaign.

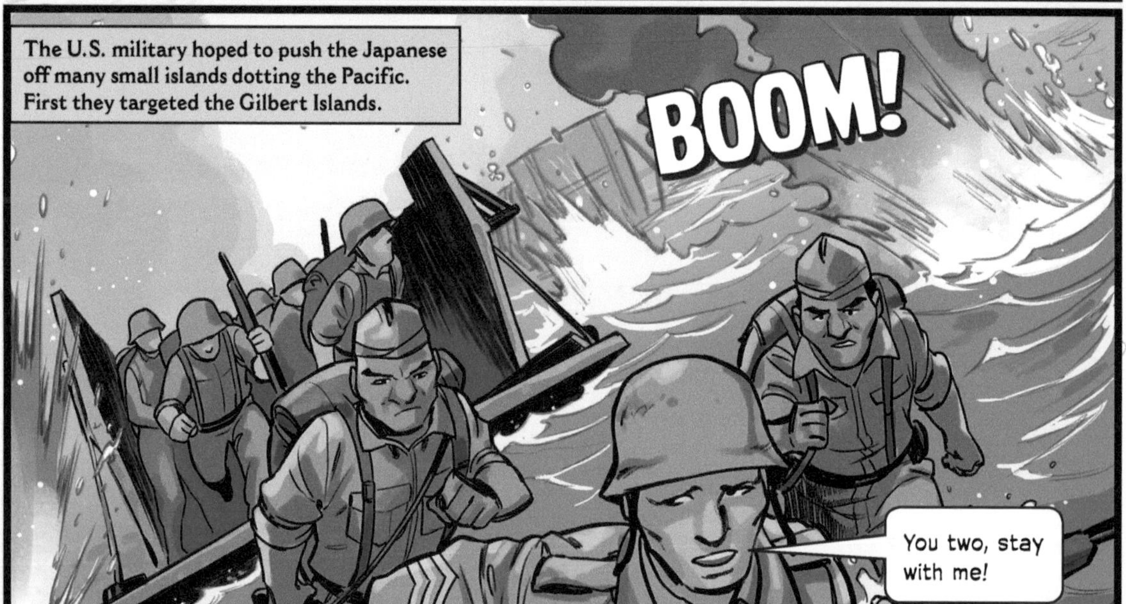
The U.S. military hoped to push the Japanese off many small islands dotting the Pacific. First they targeted the Gilbert Islands.
BOOM!
You two, stay with me!
BOOM!

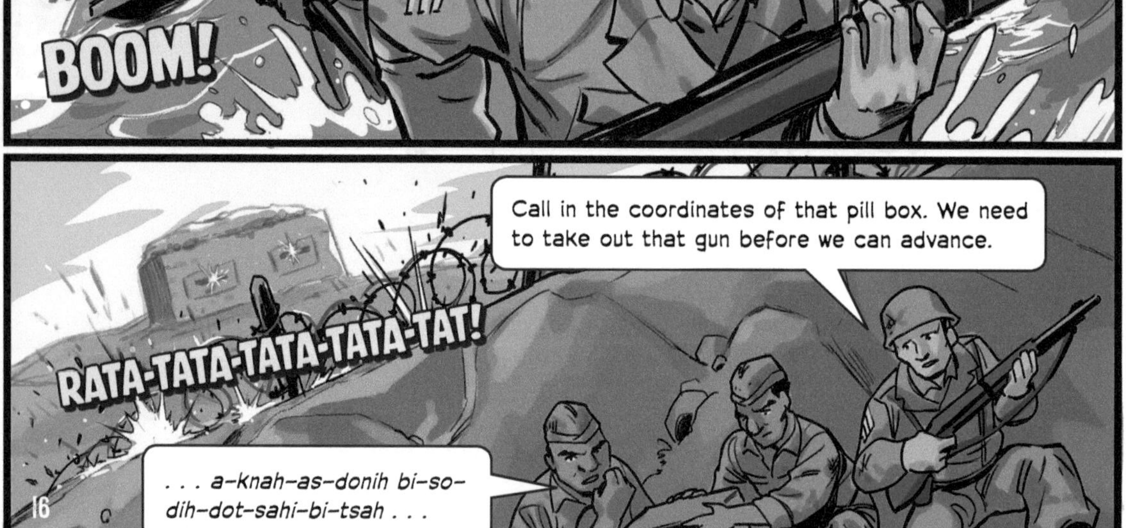
Call in the coordinates of that pill box. We need to take out that gun before we can advance.
RATA-TATA-TATA-TATA-TAT!
. . . a-knah-as-donih bi-so-dih-dot-sahi-bi-tsah . . .

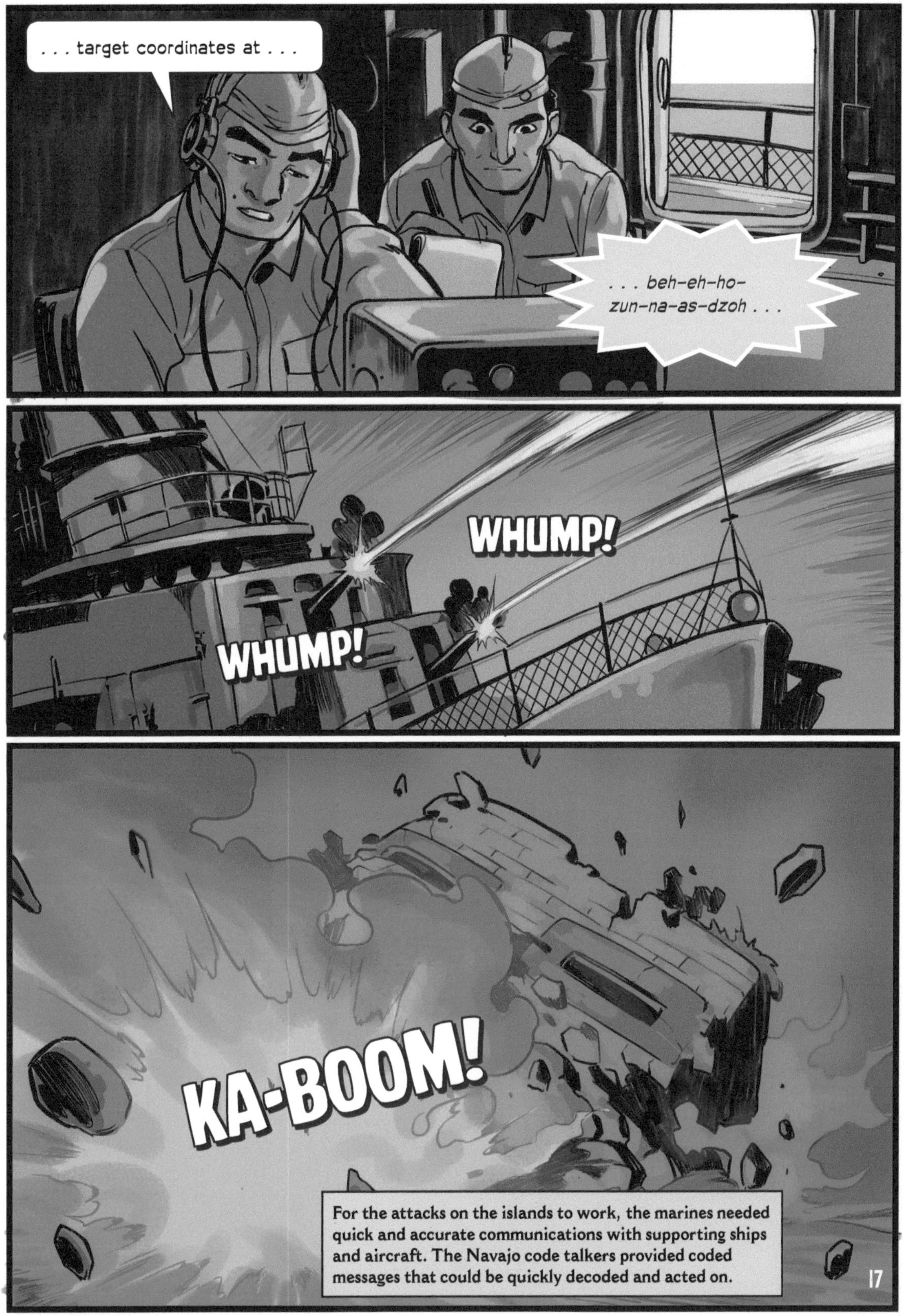
. . . target coordinates at . . .
. . . beh-eh-ho-zun-na-as-dzoh . . .
WHUMP!
WHUMP!
KA-BOOM!
For the attacks on the islands to work, the marines needed quick and accurate communications with supporting ships and aircraft. The Navajo code talkers provided coded messages that could be quickly decoded and acted on.

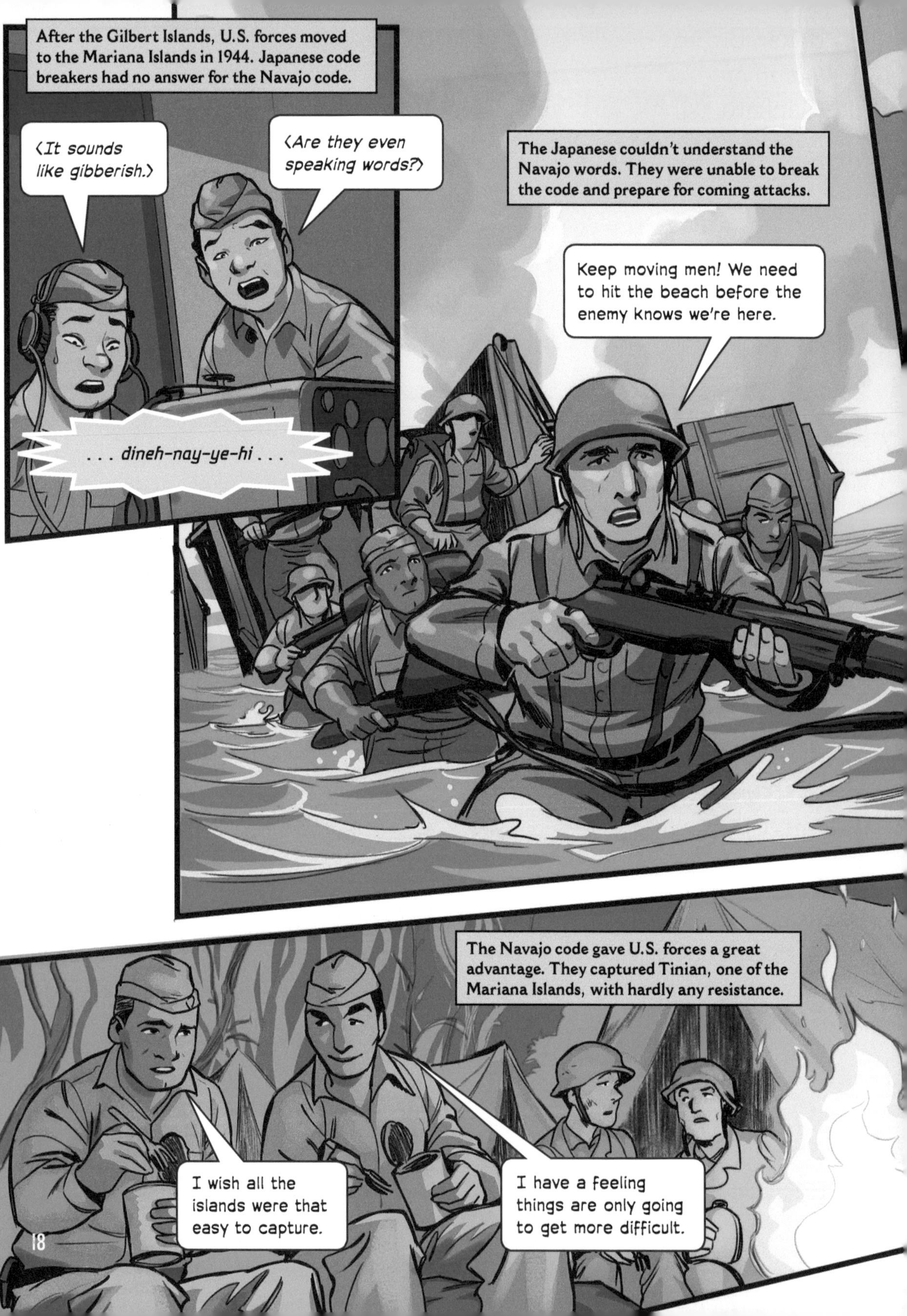
After the Gilbert Islands, U.S. forces moved to the Mariana Islands in 1944. Japanese code breakers had no answer for the Navajo code.
‹It sounds like gibberish.›
‹Are they even speaking words?›
. . . dineh-nay-ye-hi . . .
The Japanese couldn't understand the Navajo words. They were unable to break the code and prepare for coming attacks.
Keep moving men! We need to hit the beach before the enemy knows we're here.
The Navajo code gave U.S. forces a great advantage. They captured Tinian, one of the Mariana Islands, with hardly any resistance.
I wish all the islands were that easy to capture.
I have a feeling things are only going to get more difficult.

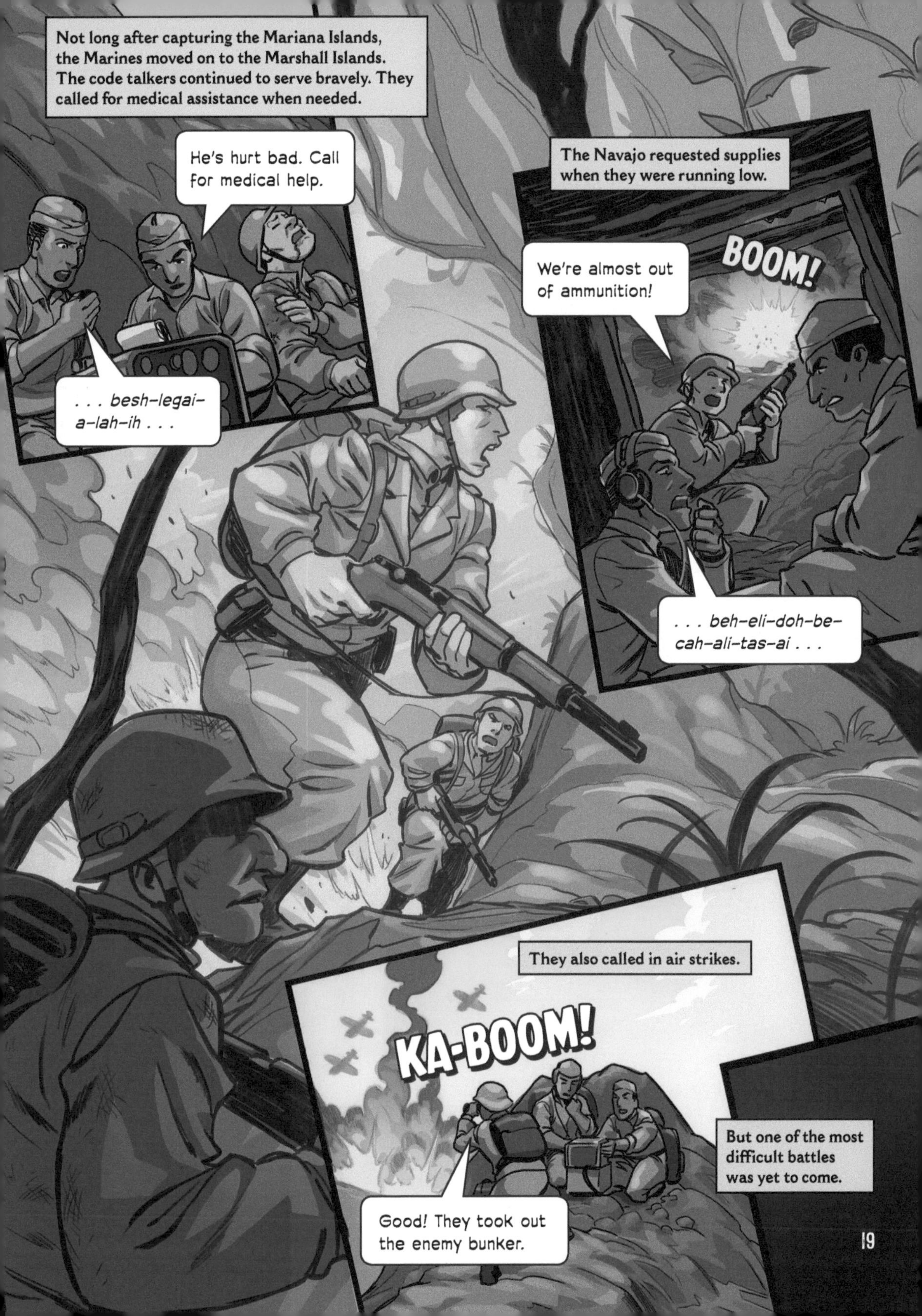
Not long after capturing the Mariana Islands, the Marines moved on to the Marshall Islands. The code talkers continued to serve bravely. They called for medical assistance when needed.
He's hurt bad. Call for medical help.
. . . besh-legai-a-lah-ih . . .
The Navajo requested supplies when they were running low.
We're almost out of ammunition!
BOOM!
. . . beh-eli-doh-be-cah-ali-tas-ai . . .
They also called in air strikes.
KA-BOOM!
Good! They took out the enemy bunker.
But one of the most difficult battles was yet to come.

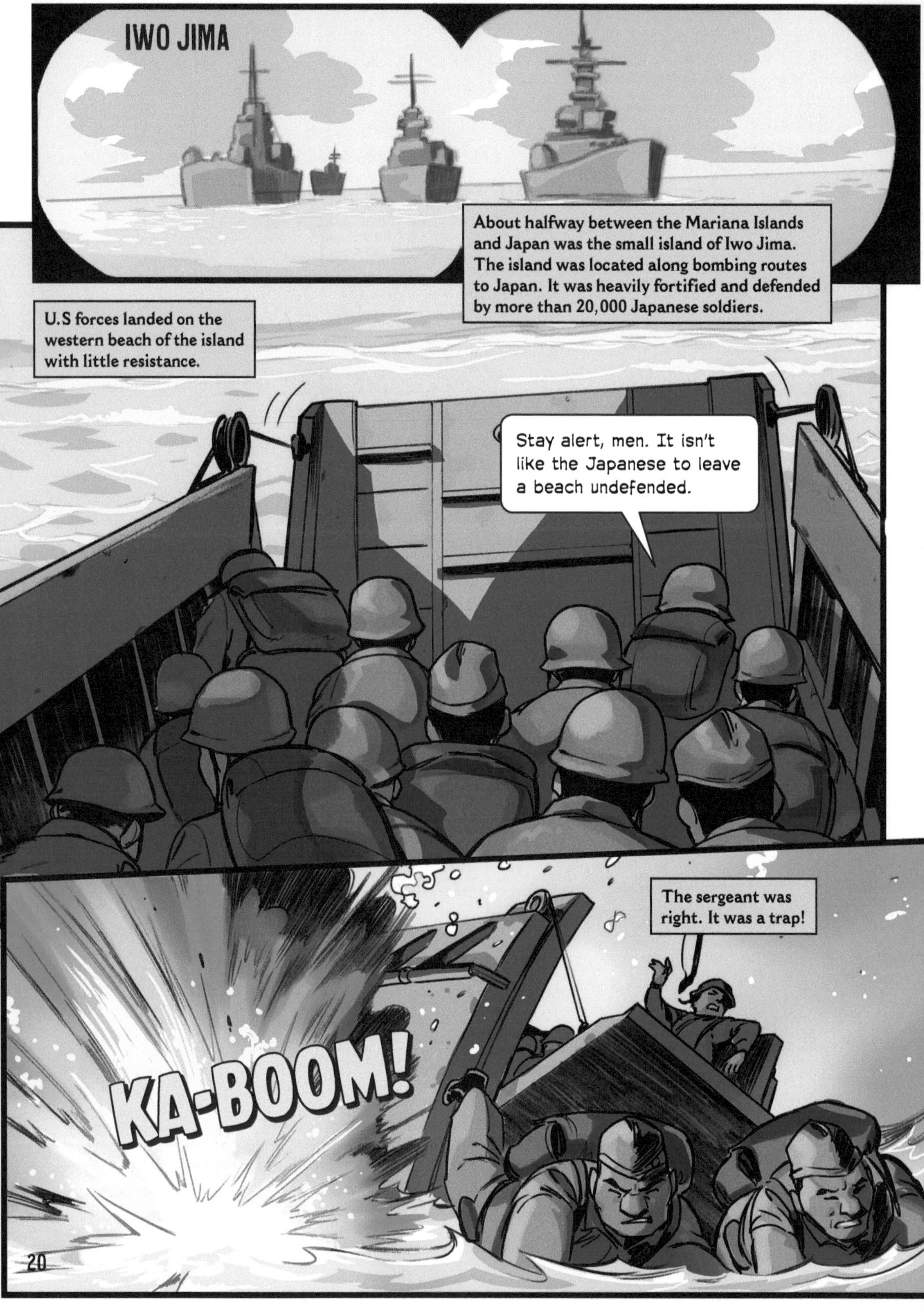
IWO JIMA
About halfway between the Mariana Islands and Japan was the small island of Iwo Jima. The island was located along bombing routes to Japan. It was heavily fortified and defended by more than 20,000 Japanese soldiers.
U.S forces landed on the western beach of the island with little resistance.
Stay alert, men. It isn't like the Japanese to leave a beach undefended.
The sergeant was right. It was a trap!
KA-BOOM!

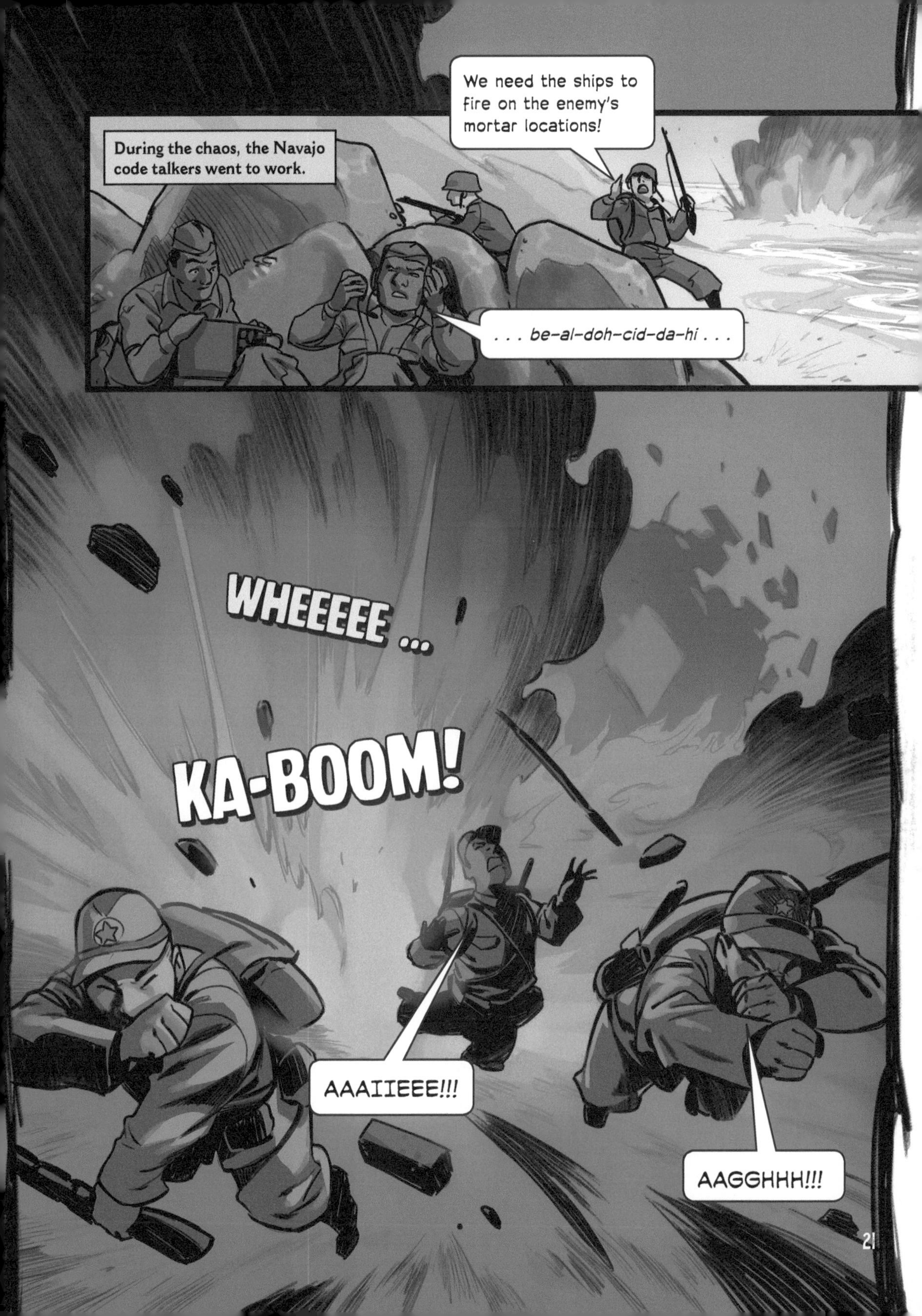
During the chaos, the Navajo code talkers went to work.
We need the ships to fire on the enemy's mortar locations!
. . . be-al-doh-cid-da-hi . . .
WHEEEEE ...
KA-BOOM!
AAAIIEEE!!!
AAGGHHH!!!

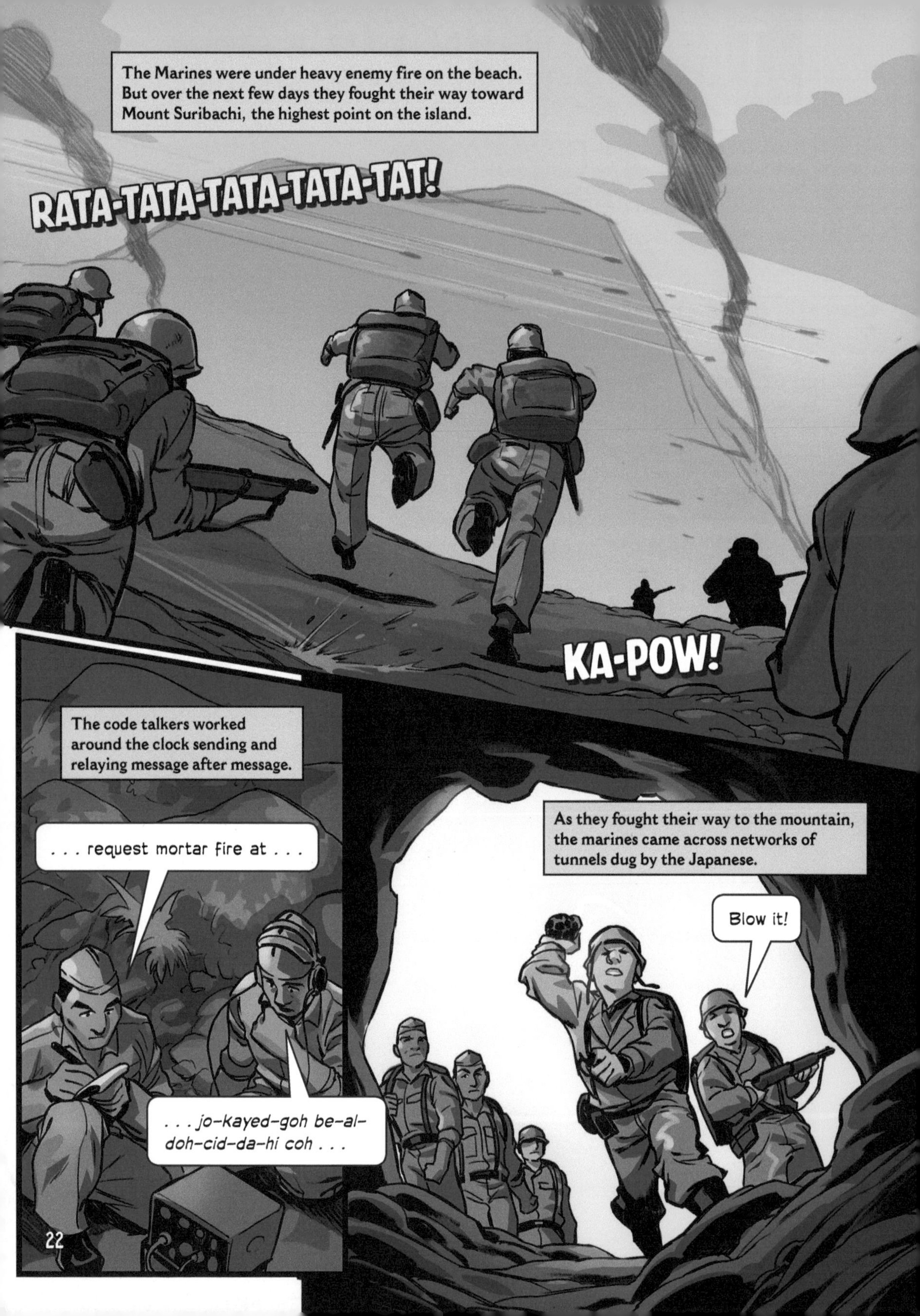
The Marines were under heavy enemy fire on the beach. But over the next few days they fought their way toward Mount Suribachi, the highest point on the island.
RATA-TATA-TATA-TATA-TAT!
KA-POW!
The code talkers worked around the clock sending and relaying message after message.
. . . request mortar fire at . . .
. . . jo-kayed-goh be-al-doh-cid-da-hi coh . . .
As they fought their way to the mountain, the marines came across networks of tunnels dug by the Japanese.
Blow it!

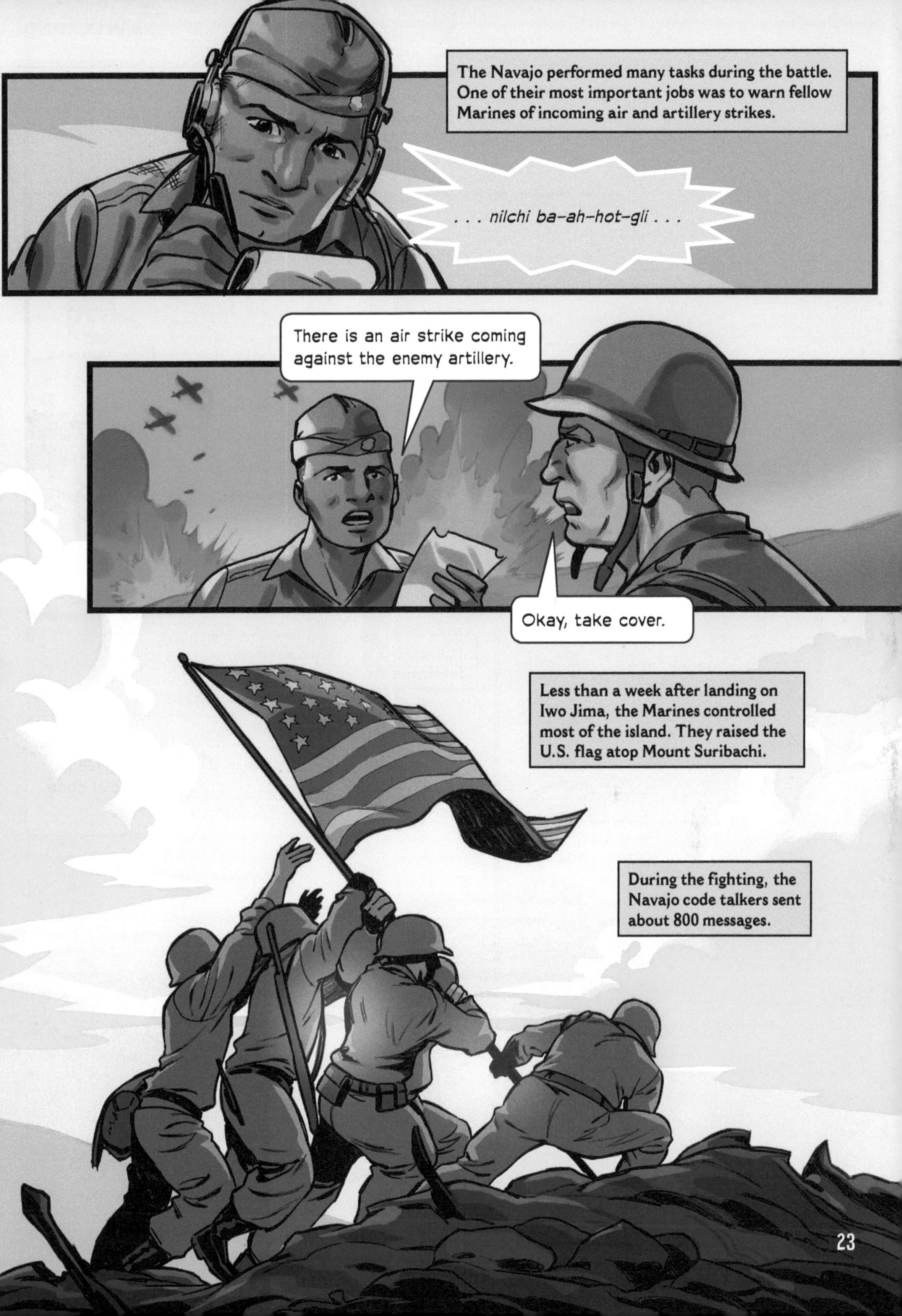
The Navajo performed many tasks during the battle. One of their most important jobs was to warn fellow Marines of incoming air and artillery strikes.
. . . nilchi ba-ah-hot-gli . . .
There is an air strike coming against the enemy artillery.
Okay, take cover.
Less than a week after landing on Iwo Jima, the Marines controlled most of the island. They raised the U.S. flag atop Mount Suribachi.
During the fighting, the Navajo code talkers sent about 800 messages.

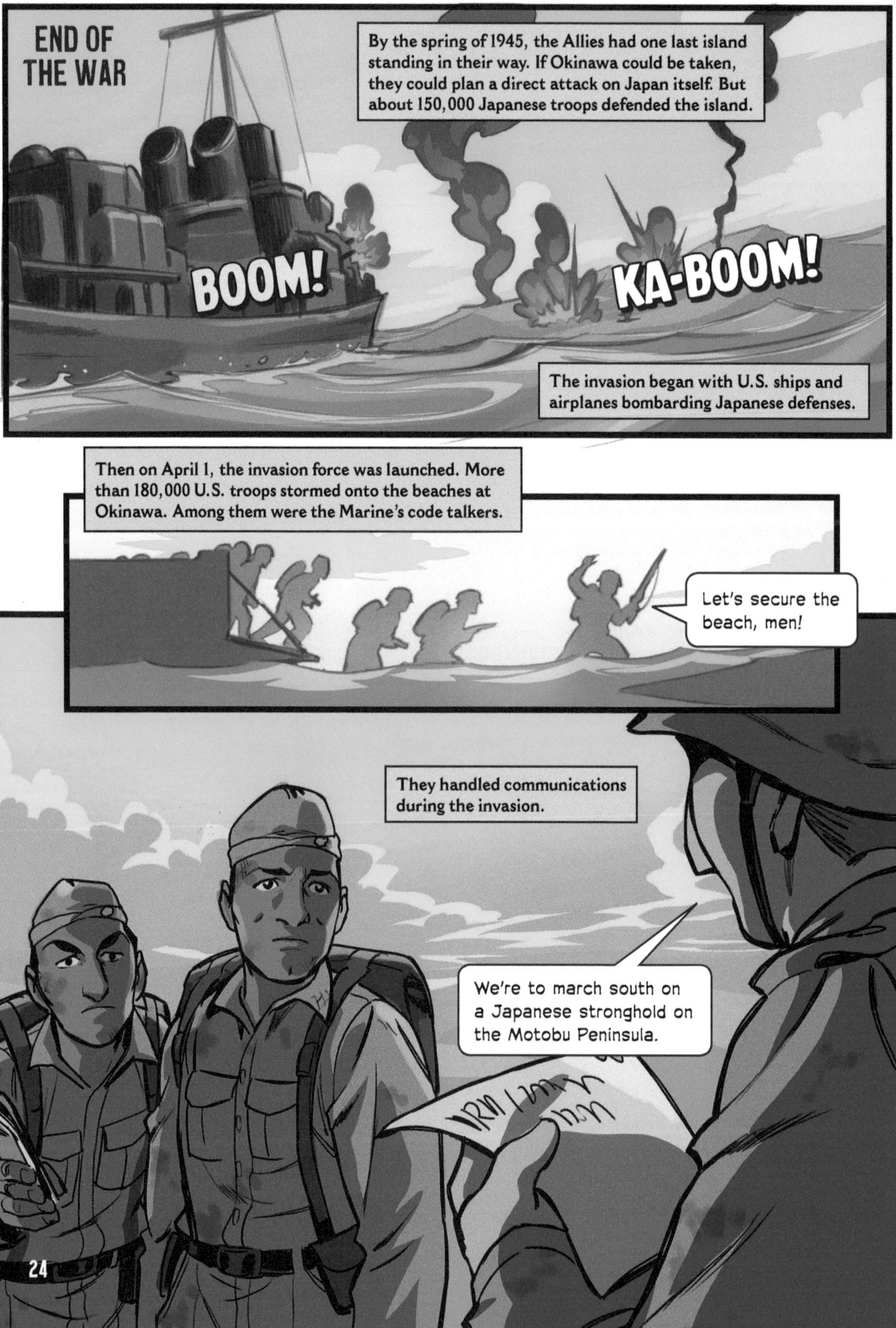
END OF THE WAR
By the spring of 1945, the Allies had one last island standing in their way. If Okinawa could be taken, they could plan a direct attack on Japan itself. But about 150,000 Japanese troops defended the island.
BOOM!
KA-BOOM!
The invasion began with U.S. ships and airplanes bombarding Japanese defenses.
Then on April 1, the invasion force was launched. More than 180,000 U.S. troops stormed onto the beaches at Okinawa. Among them were the Marine's code talkers.
Let's secure the beach, men!
They handled communications during the invasion.
We're to march south on a Japanese stronghold on the Motobu Peninsula.

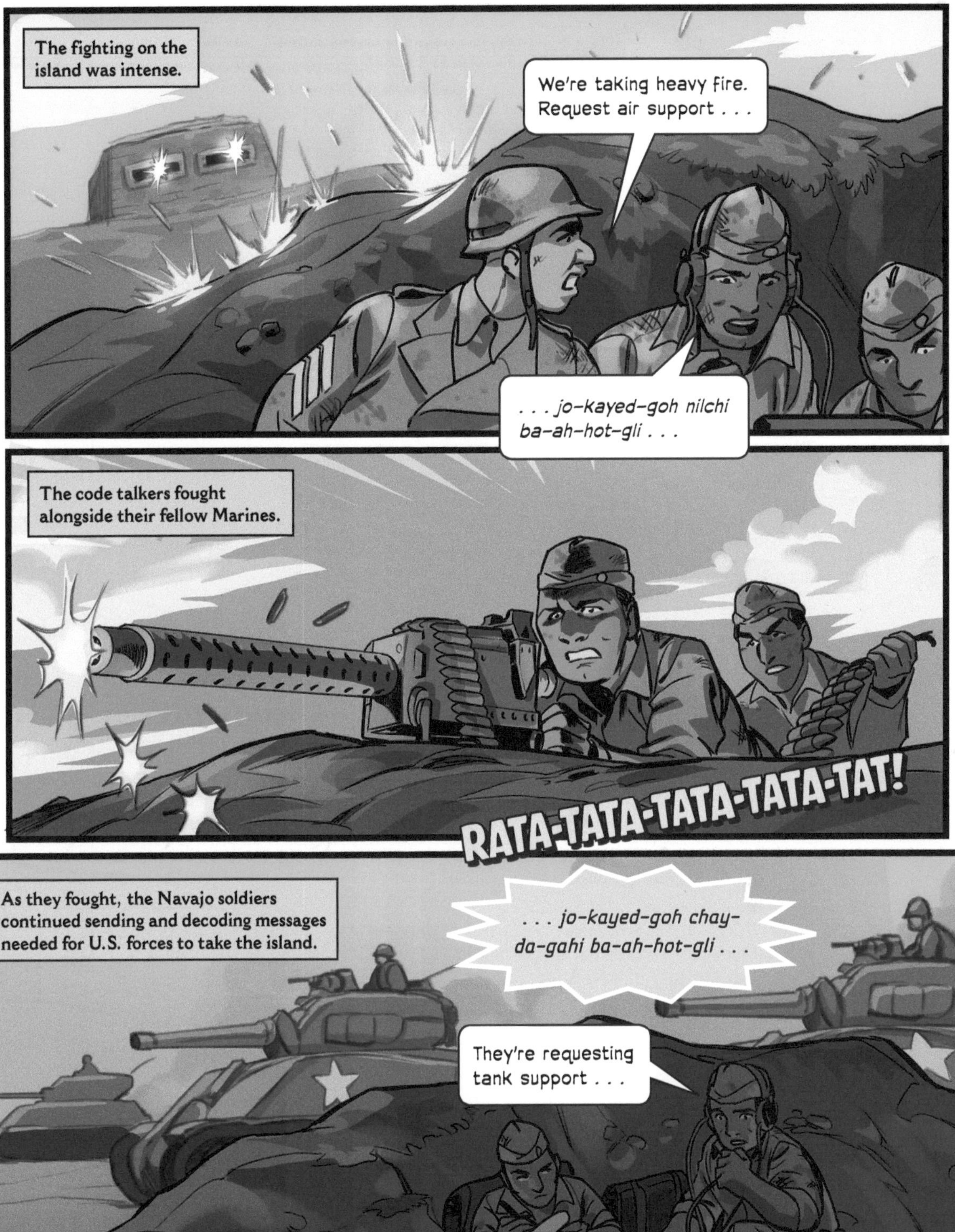
The fighting on the island was intense.
We're taking heavy fire. Request air support . . .
. . . jo-kayed-goh nilchi ba-ah-hot-gli . . .
The code talkers fought alongside their fellow Marines.
RATA-TATA-TATA-TATA-TAT!
As they fought, the Navajo soldiers continued sending and decoding messages needed for U.S. forces to take the island.
. . . jo-kayed-goh chay-da-gahi ba-ah-hot-gli . . .
They're requesting tank support . . .
While the fighting raged on in the Pacific, Nazi forces surrendered to the Allies in May, 1945. The only Axis Power still fighting was Japan. A month later, Allied forces would take control of Okinawa.

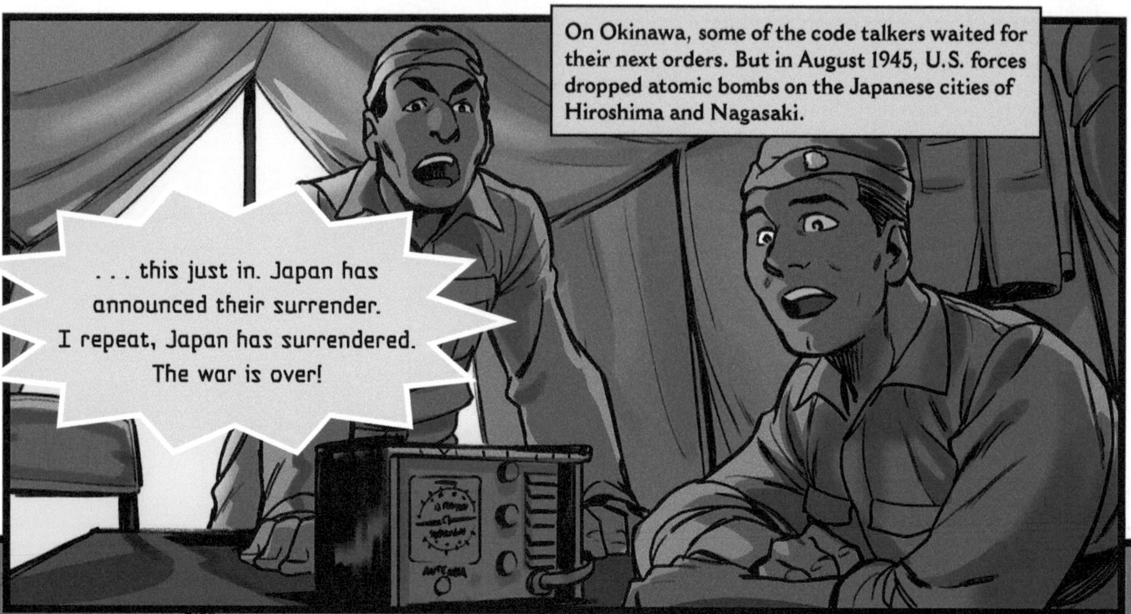
On Okinawa, some of the code talkers waited for their next orders. But in August 1945, U.S. forces dropped atomic bombs on the Japanese cities of Hiroshima and Nagasaki.
. . . this just in. Japan has announced their surrender. I repeat, Japan has surrendered. The war is over!

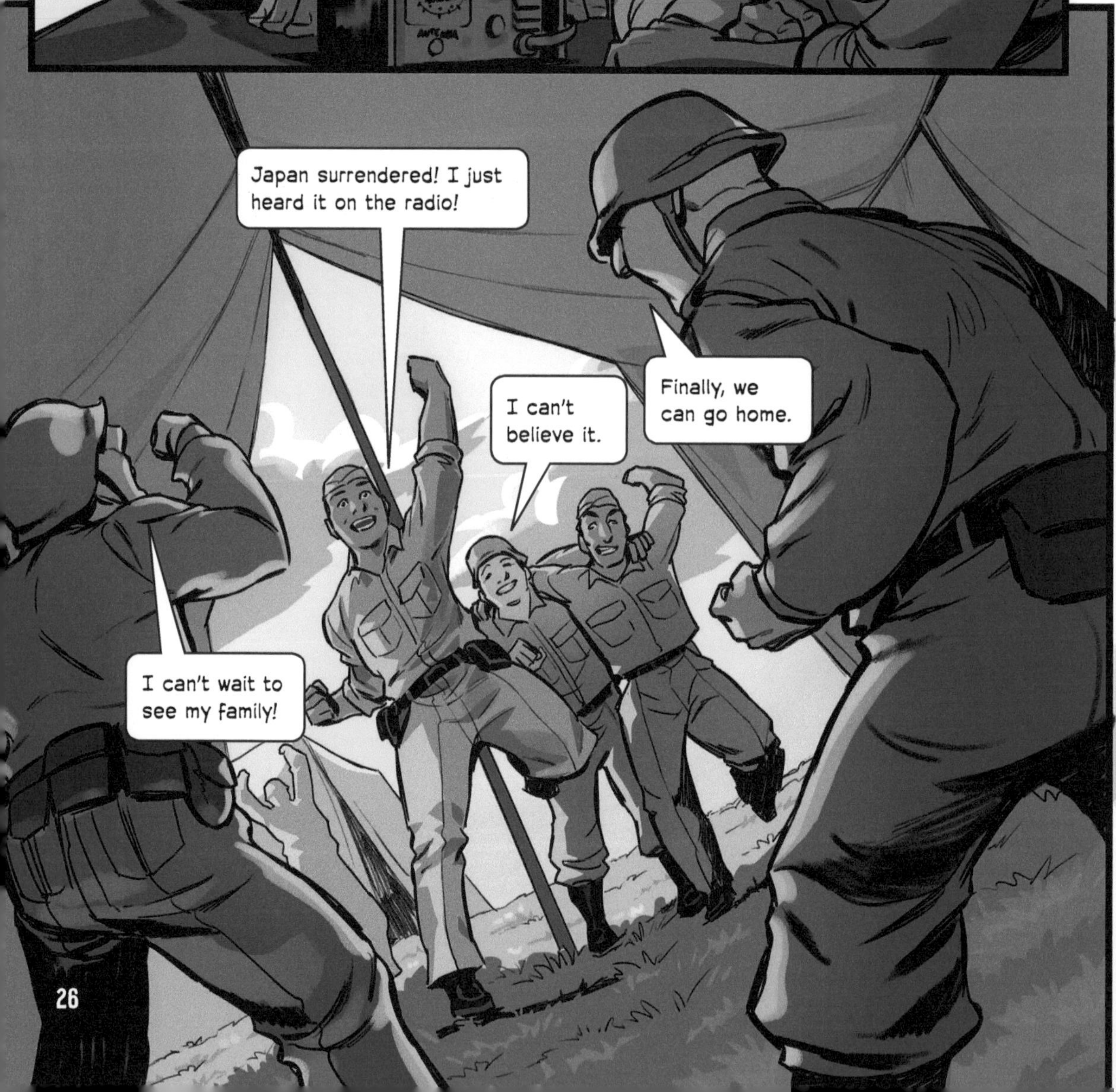
Japan surrendered! I just heard it on the radio!
I can't believe it.
Finally, we can go home.
I can't wait to see my family!

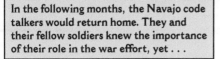

In the following months, the Navajo code talkers would return home. They and their fellow soldiers knew the importance of their role in the war effort, yet . . .

The Navajo code must be kept a secret. We may need it in future conflicts. You will not speak of it or your missions to anyone. Is that clear?

Yes, sir.

27

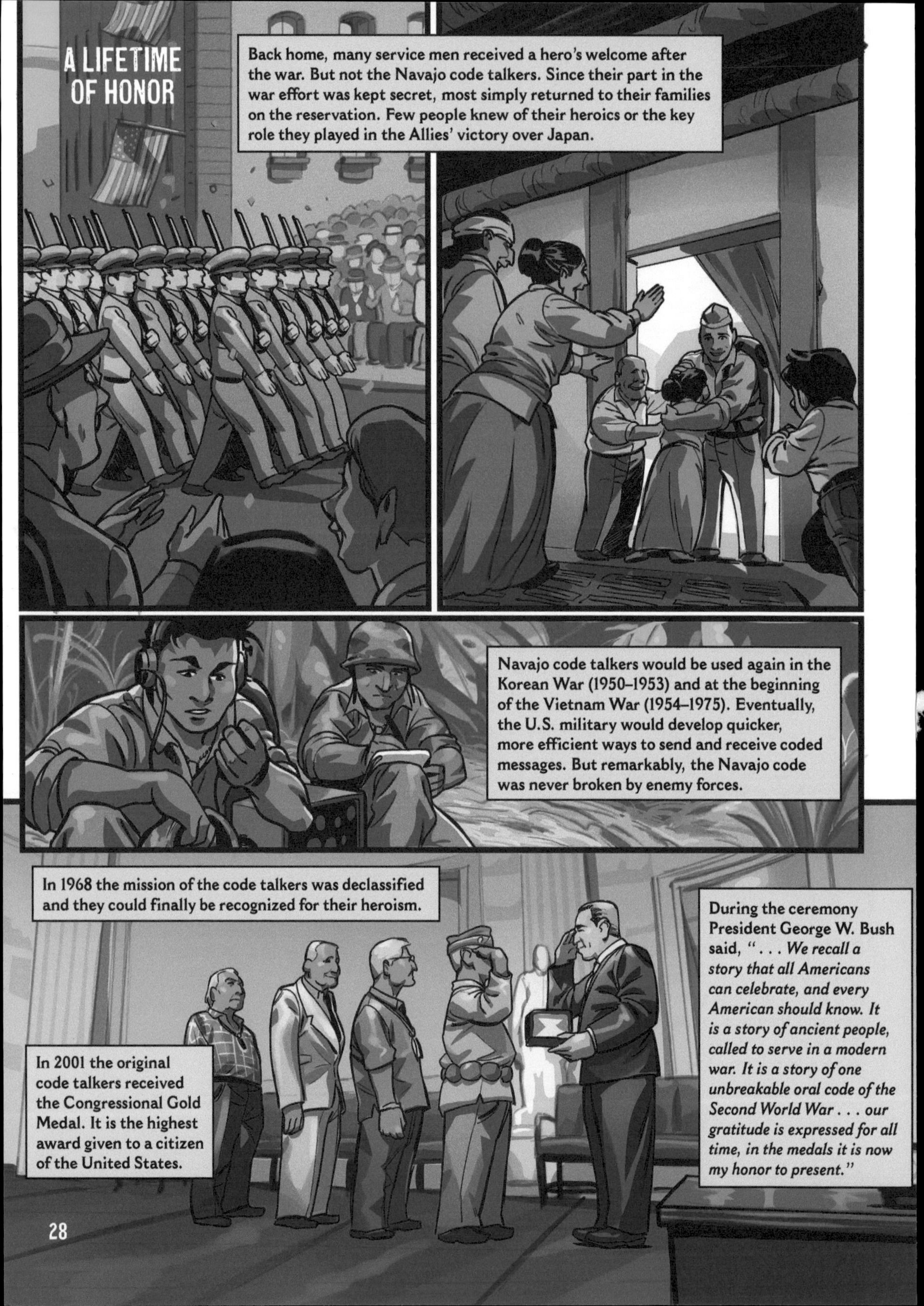

A LIFETIME OF HONOR

Back home, many service men received a hero's welcome after the war. But not the Navajo code talkers. Since their part in the war effort was kept secret, most simply returned to their families on the reservation. Few people knew of their heroics or the key role they played in the Allies' victory over Japan.

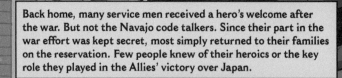

Navajo code talkers would be used again in the Korean War (1950–1953) and at the beginning of the Vietnam War (1954–1975). Eventually, the U.S. military would develop quicker, more efficient ways to send and receive coded messages. But remarkably, the Navajo code was never broken by enemy forces.

In 1968 the mission of the code talkers was declassified and they could finally be recognized for their heroism.

In 2001 the original code talkers received the Congressional Gold Medal. It is the highest award given to a citizen of the United States.

During the ceremony President George W. Bush said, " . . . We recall a story that all Americans can celebrate, and every American should know. It is a story of ancient people, called to serve in a modern war. It is a story of one unbreakable oral code of the Second World War . . . our gratitude is expressed for all time, in the medals it is now my honor to present."

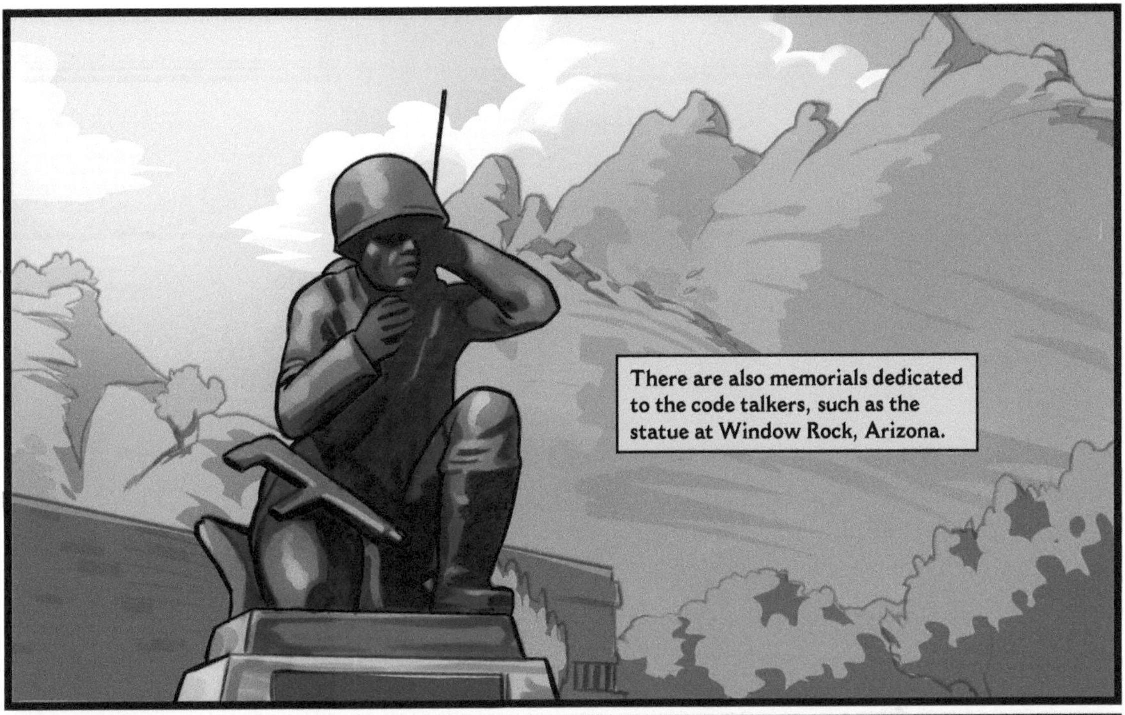
There are also memorials dedicated to the code talkers, such as the statue at Window Rock, Arizona.

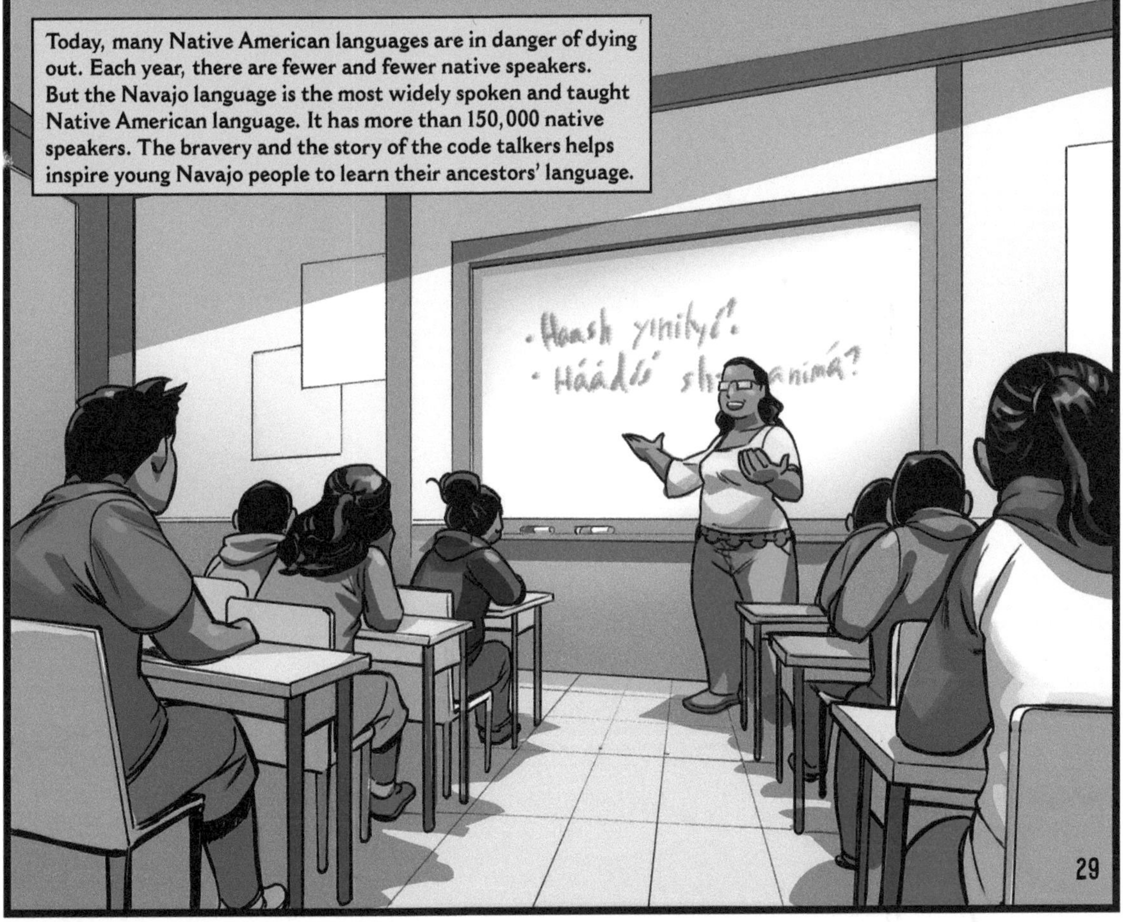
Today, many Native American languages are in danger of dying out. Each year, there are fewer and fewer native speakers. But the Navajo language is the most widely spoken and taught Native American language. It has more than 150,000 native speakers. The bravery and the story of the code talkers helps inspire young Navajo people to learn their ancestors' language.

GLOSSARY

Allies (AL-lyz)—the group of countries that fought against the Axis powers in World War II, including the United States, Great Britain, France, and the Soviet Union

artillery (ar-TIL-uh-ree)—cannons and other large guns designed to strike an enemy from a distance

Axis powers (AK-siss POU-urz)—the group of countries that fought against the Allies in World War II, including Japan, Germany, and Italy

coordinates (koh-OR-duh-nits)—a set of numbers used to show the position of a point on a map

decipher (di-SYE-fur)—to figure out something that is written in a code

declassify (dee-KLAS-uh-fahy)—to make secret documents or information open to public knowledge

Pacific Theater (puh-SIF-ik THEE-uh-tur)—the area in the Pacific Ocean in which several battles took place between the United States and Japan during World War II

recruit (ri-KROOT)—a new member of the armed forces

reservation (rez-ur-VAY-shuhn)—an area of land set aside by the U.S. government for American Indians

treaty (TREE-tee)—an official agreement between two or more countries to help each other and work together

READ MORE

Baker, Brynn. *Navajo Code Talkers: Secret American Indian Heroes of World War II.* Military Heroes. North Mankato, MN: Capstone Press, 2016.

Owens, Lisa L. *World War II Code Breakers*. Heroes of World War II. Minneapolis: Lerner Publications, 2019.

Shoup, Kate. *Life as a Navajo Code Talker.* New York: Cavendish Square Publishing, 2018.

CRITICAL THINKING QUESTIONS

- The Navajo code often used words for other objects that seemed similar. For example, the Navajo word for 'tortoise' described a tank. What code words could you use to describe objects like books, sports equipment, or a video game? Create your own code dictionary and try using your code to send secret messages to your friends.

- The Navajo soldiers were not allowed to talk about the code or their achievements during the war. How do you think they felt when their fellow soldiers were honored for their war efforts, but they were not?

- Imagine that the Axis had won World War II instead of the Allies. The western United States would likely be controlled by Japan. Meanwhile, Germany would rule the eastern states. Imagine how your life would be different. Depending on where you live, what different things might you learn in school, eat, and do?

INTERNET SITES

National Museum of the American Indian: Code Talkers
https://americanindian.si.edu/education/codetalkers/html/chapter4.html

Navajo Code Talkers and the Unbreakable Code
https://www.cia.gov/news-information/featured-story-archive/2008-featured-story-archive/navajo-code-talkers/

Naval History and Heritage Command: Navajo Code Talkers' Dictionary
https://www.history.navy.mil/research/library/online-reading-room/title-list-alphabetically/n/navajo-code-talker-dictionary.html

INDEX